OCCASIONAL PAPER 124

Saving Behavior and the Asset Price "Bubble" in Japan

Analytical Studies

Edited by Ulrich Baumgartner and Guy Meredith, with a staff team comprising Juha Kähkönen, Kenneth Miranda, Garry J. Schinasi, and Alexander W. Hoffmaister

INTERNATIONAL MONETARY FUND

Washington DC

April 1995

© 1995 International Monetary Fund

Library of Congress Cataloging-in-Publication Data

Saving behavior and the asset price "bubble" in Japan : analytical studies /
Ulrich Baumgartner, Guy Meredith ; with a staff team comprising Juha
Kähkönen . . . [et al.].
  p. cm. — (Occasional Papers, ISSN 0251-6365 ; no. 124)
  Includes bibliographical references.
  ISBN 1-55775-462-4
  1. Saving and investment—Japan. 2. Stocks—Prices—Japan.
3. Financial crises—Japan. 4. Japan—Economic conditions—
1945–1989. I. Baumgartner, Ulrich, 1946– . II. Meredith, Guy.
III. Kähkönen, Juha. IV. Series: Occasional paper (International
Monetary Fund) ; no. 124.
HC465.S3S25 1995
332.63'222'0952—dc20   95-10141
                 CIP

Price: US$15.00
(US$12.00 to full-time faculty members and
students at universities and colleges)

Please send orders to:
International Monetary Fund, Publication Services
700 19th Street, N.W., Washington, D.C. 20431, U.S.A.
Tel.: (202) 623-7430   Telefax: (202) 623-7201
Internet: publications@imf.org

recycled paper

Contents

Tables

Charts

The following symbols have been used throughout this paper:

. . .   to indicate that data are not available;

—   to indicate that the figure is zero or less than half the final digit shown, or that the item does not exist;

–   between years or months (for example, 1991–92 or January–June) to indicate the years or months covered, including the beginning and ending years or months;

/   between years or months (for example, 1991/92) to indicate a crop or fiscal (financial) year.

"Billion" means a thousand million; "trillion" means a thousand billion.

Minor discrepancies between constituent figures and totals are due to rounding.

The term "country," as used in this paper, does not in all cases refer to a territorial entity that is a state as understood by international law and practice; the term also covers some territorial entities that are not states, but for which statistical data are maintained and provided internationally on a separate and independent basis.

Preface

This Occasional Paper is based on research papers prepared in connection with the IMF's recent Article IV consultations with Japan. The authors are grateful for the cooperation of the Japanese authorities in the preparation of these studies. They would also like to thank Bijan B. Aghevli for his encouragement and support of the project, and Daniel Citrin, Yusuke Horiguchi, Kenji Okamura, Chikahisa Sumi, and Christopher Towe for their valuable comments. Thanks are also due to Harish Mendis and Toh Kuan for research assistance, and to Elizabeth Elliott, Prabha Job, and Tammy Shear for secretarial support. James McEuen of the External Relations Department edited the paper for publication and coordinated production. The views expressed here, as well as any errors, are the sole responsibility of the authors and do not necessarily reflect the opinions of the Government of Japan, Executive Directors of the IMF, or other members of the IMF staff.

I Overview

Ulrich Baumgartner and Guy Meredith

This volume brings together various analytical studies the IMF staff has undertaken on the Japanese economy, focusing on two areas of particular interest for both longer-term economic performance and recent cyclical developments. The first is Japan's saving behavior; the second is the remarkable swing in asset prices that occurred in the late 1980s and early 1990s. As regards saving, Japan for many years has had the highest national saving rate among the major industrial countries. While its domestic investment rate has also been higher than that of other major industrial countries, the excess of saving over investment has been reflected in Japan's significant current account surplus since the early 1980s. Japan's saving performance raises several issues. Does Japan save "too much" on economic grounds? How has Japan's saving been channeled abroad? What effect will an aging population have on future saving patterns of the private and public sectors? Answers to these questions are the focus of Sections II through V of this volume.

Section II considers whether Japan's saving can be characterized as excessively high. To address this issue, Kenneth Miranda invokes three criteria—based on "golden rule," dynamic efficiency, and marginal productivity conditions—to shed light on whether a country is over- or undersaving. The golden-rule approach allows calculation of the optimal level of saving based on parameters for productivity and population growth, capital depreciation, the capital share in output, and the social rate of time preference. In practice, the rate of time preference cannot be observed directly but is inferred from observed saving data and the other parameters. The evidence is consistent with a rate of time preference ranging from ½ of 1 percent to 2 percent a year, suggesting that the assumption of abnormal rates of time preference is not needed to explain Japanese saving. The dynamic efficiency approach, in contrast, provides a nonparametric test of whether a country is oversaving: if investment, on average, exceeds the share of profits in output, then long-run consumption possibilities could be increased by reducing saving. For Japan, the investment rate has averaged less than the share of profits in gross national product (GNP) since the mid-1970s, indicating that the economy has operated in a dynamically efficient range. Finally, marginal productivity tests assess whether the return to capital has exceeded alternative estimates of

the opportunity cost of capital: again, results suggest that capital is unlikely to have been overaccumulated. All of these indicators of excess saving are subject to caveats, but they provide a broad range of evidence against the proposition that Japanese saving has been inefficiently high.

Section III, by Juha Kähkönen, analyzes developments in Japan's capital flows since 1980. Japan has been the world's largest exporter of capital over this period, despite having the highest domestic investment rate among major industrial countries. Trends in Japan's capital account since 1980 can be divided into three phases. In the first half of the 1980s, the liberalization of external capital flows coincided with a surge in long-term capital outflows, especially of portfolio investment. In the second half of the decade, further steps toward financial liberalization—both external and domestic—as well as the surge in asset prices led to a further rise in long-term capital outflow, financed in part by short-term external borrowing. The share of foreign direct investment (FDI) in Japan's capital exports increased sharply during this period because appreciation of the yen made overseas investment more attractive. These developments were reversed in the early 1990s. The collapse of the asset price bubble and the introduction of Bank for International Settlements capital-adequacy guidelines led to a sharp retrenchment by financial institutions—short-term foreign liabilities were repaid by sales of long-term assets, causing long-term capital exports to fall. At the same time, the economic downturn reduced corporate profits and led to a sharp rise in excess domestic capacity, reducing the attractiveness of FDI. The section continues with a more detailed exploration of the composition of Japan's FDI and its effects on other countries. Both structural factors (such as evolving comparative advantage) and macroeconomic developments have played important roles in driving FDI. The benefits to other countries consist not only of the usual gains from international integration, but also of positive spillovers in the form of new technology and organizational skills.

Sections IV and V deal with the potential impact of an aging population on Japan's saving rate. In Section IV Guy Meredith assesses the effect on saving behavior at the household level, and in Section V he presents a simulation analysis of the impact on aggregate public and private saving. Population aging is an important issue for Japan because of the projected size of the demographic shift in coming years: during 1990–2020, Japan is expected to experience the sharpest increase in its "old-age dependency ratio" (the ratio of the elderly to the working-age population) among the major industrial countries. As discussed in Section IV, if households behave in accordance with life-cycle consumption theory, private saving will fall as the share of the elderly—who are net dissavers—in the population rises in relation to that of other segments of the population. The magnitude of this effect has been questioned by some observers, however, because some microeconomic data suggest that the saving rate of the elderly is not significantly different from that of working-age households. The analysis in this section shows that, when properly measured, the saving rate of the elderly is indeed well below that of working-age households. Furthermore, shifts in demographic structure will generate changes in the saving rates of individual population cohorts through their effect on public pension contribution and benefit rates. The overall impact of population aging on the aggregate saving rate is quantified through simulations of a life-cycle model of household behavior. The results suggest that the household saving rate will decline significantly as a result of population aging, although the drop may not be as large as some studies using macroeconomic data have indicated.

Section V provides a long-run simulation analysis of the effects of population aging. Particular emphasis is placed on the impact of rising pension benefits and increased health care on public sector saving. In this context, Japan is often regarded as having a relatively healthy fiscal situation, in large part because of the substantial surplus in the social security system. The analysis shows, however, that, in the absence of pension reform, a social security deficit would emerge by early in the next decade; by 2025, the deficit on social security could amount to almost 15 percent of gross domestic product (GDP). Combined with the government deficit on operations not related to the social security system, this implies a substantial financing "gap" that will have to be filled by a combination of pension reform, higher taxes, and reduced spending on other government operations—or a combination of these—if an explosive rise in government debt is to be avoided. Part of this gap could be filled by the enactment of a tax reform package that would offset the loss in revenues from the 1994 income tax cut. In addition, the implementation of recent reforms to the pension system will play an important role in addressing the fiscal imbalance. Nevertheless, simulations show that further measures will need to be taken to put Japan's fiscal position on a sustainable footing. From the point of view of the overall economy, a sharp drop in public saving, combined with a demographically induced decline in private saving, would cause a sharp swing in the external surplus in coming years.

The second area analyzed in this volume is asset price developments, during both the 1987–90 "bubble" period and the subsequent economic downturn. The boom in Japan's equity and land prices during the bubble was accompanied by an extraordinary surge in private spending, especially on business investment. Output rose well above its supply capacity, leading to inflationary pressures in product markets, while the current account surplus declined sharply in relation to GDP. In the event, both the inflated level of asset prices and the boom in spending were abruptly reversed in the early 1990s, causing one of the longest and deepest recessions in postwar history. These developments and their effects are analyzed in Sections VI and VII.

Section VI, by Juha Kähkönen, describes the evolution of asset prices during and after the bubble period, assesses the role played by various factors in driving asset prices during this episode, and provides estimates of their effect on real activity. On the basis of equations summarizing the behavior of equity and land prices in the period preceding the bubble, it is it is shown that changes in "fundamentals"—such as economic growth rates, monetary policy, and corporate earnings—can explain at least part of the surge in asset prices during the late 1980s. Greater risk taking, owing to changes in the financial environment, and distortions in Japan's land tax system may also have played contributing roles. But there remains an unexplained component of asset price movements, consistent with the view that speculative forces carried prices beyond the level consistent with underlying determinants. In terms of private spending, an important channel was the effect on investment of increased market valuation of the capital stock, which could have raised capital spending by about 10 percent in the late 1980s. Higher land prices may also have eased corporate borrowing constraints by raising collateral values. The effect on private consumption was smaller, since Japanese households are not large holders of corporate equities, and changes in land prices are estimated to have only a minor effect on consumption. Similarly, the surge in land prices does not appear to have driven the boom in residential construction.

In Section VII, Alex Hoffmaister and Garry Schinasi examine the relationship between macroeconomic variables and asset price inflation in the 1980s. The focus is on land price inflation, rather than on stock price movements; although stock prices are difficult to model empirically, land prices generally move systematically in response to changes in economic fundamentals. Several related questions are investigated: (1) whether there was a structural break in the way monetary factors affected asset prices in the 1980s; (2) whether monetary factors contributed to asset price inflation in important ways in the 1980s; (3) factors responsible for the divergent behavior of asset prices and consumer prices; and (4) whether there is support for the view that the effects of monetary factors were "concentrated" in asset markets rather than in goods markets. Strong evidence is found for a shift in the relationships between monetary factors and land prices in the early 1980s: in particular, the parameters imply a much more important channel of transmission in the second part of the sample than in the first. A key conclusion is that monetary shocks led to more asset price inflation (and less consumer price infla-tion) in the 1984–93 period than during 1970–83. This "regime shift"—which is largely attributed to the effects of financial liberalization—made it difficult to interpret the factors underlying the rise in asset prices in the late 1980s, perhaps explaining why policymakers did not fully perceive the implications of allowing the bubble to continue as long as it did.

II Does Japan Save Too Much?

Kenneth Miranda

Japan's high saving rate relative to those of other industrial countries gives rise to the question of whether Japan is saving "too much." This section utilizes the conditions on optimal steady-state saving behavior derived from neoclassical growth theory to examine whether Japan saves too much (or too little)—thus assessing the optimality of its national saving behavior.

The section is organized as follows: the first part provides a brief review of recent trends in Japanese saving behavior and a comparison with other major industrial countries; following an outline of three testable conditions derived from neoclassical growth theory for assessing the sufficiency of saving, the second part examines the empirical evidence for each of these approaches; the last part draws some conclusions from the analysis.

How Much Does Japan Save?

Saving behavior is important because it helps to determine the evolution of future consumption opportunities. As such, saving can be viewed as the portion of current income that allows a nation to raise its future consumption opportunities—that is, to raise its standard of living.

Japan's postwar saving behavior can be viewed in this light. Saving has enabled Japan to increase its stock of assets rapidly (physical and financial as well as domestic and international), increase worker productivity, achieve rapid rates of economic growth, and raise its standard of living.

Recent Trends in National Saving

Chart 2-1 shows Japan's national saving rate, both gross and net of depreciation, for the period 1975–93. Both of these measures indicate a negative trend through the first part of the 1980s, with levels in the early 1980s that are about 2 percentage points of GNP lower than those recorded at the beginning of the period. Since 1983, however, there has been a moderate increase in saving rates.

Gross saving in Japan declined from about 33 percent of GNP in 1975 to 30 percent in 1983, before recovering beginning in the mid-1980s. Preliminary data for 1993 suggest that gross saving rebounded to 33 percent of

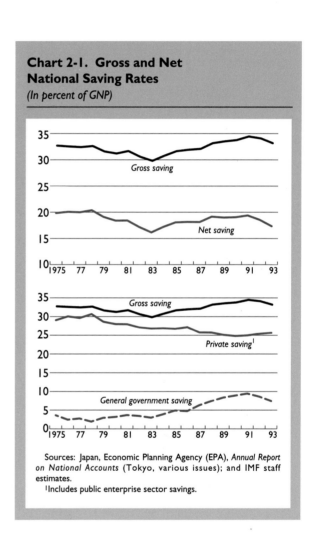

Chart 2-1. Gross and Net National Saving Rates
(In percent of GNP)

Sources: Japan, Economic Planning Agency (EPA), *Annual Report on National Accounts* (Tokyo, various issues); and IMF staff estimates.
[1]Includes public enterprise sector savings.

GNP. For net saving, the secular decline through 1983 is more marked (from 20 percent of GNP in 1976 to 16 percent of GNP by 1983) because of rapid rates of depreciation charges over the period. Chart 2-1 also shows disaggregated saving data. As can be seen, the upturn in the saving rate in the latter half of the 1980s was due primarily to an increase in general government saving.

Table 2-1. Saving Rates of Major Industrial Countries
(In percent of GNP)

	1984	1985	1986	1987	1988	1989	1990	1991	1992	1993	Average 1984–93
Canada	21.1	20.1	19.0	20.2	20.6	20.1	17.4	15.8	15.0	15.3	18.5
France	18.8	18.7	19.8	19.3	20.8	21.6	21.3	20.6	19.7	18.2	19.9
Germany	21.7	22.0	23.8	23.4	24.2	25.6	24.3	22.0	21.9	20.7	22.9
Italy	21.1	20.4	20.1	19.7	19.9	19.7	19.4	18.3	17.5	18.2	19.4
Japan	30.8	31.6	31.9	32.1	33.2	33.5	33.7	34.4	34.1	33.2	32.8
United Kingdom	17.6	17.7	16.6	16.7	16.7	16.5	15.8	14.6	13.7	13.2	15.9
United States	16.7	15.1	13.4	13.6	14.3	14.1	12.9	12.3	11.6	12.6	13.7

Source: IMF, *World Economic Outlook* (Washington, various issues).

Japanese Saving in an International Context

Table 2-1 and Chart 2-2 show Japanese gross saving in comparison with other major industrial countries for the most recent ten-year period. As can be seen, there are wide disparities in saving behavior across countries. Japan is clearly the highest saver among the major industrial countries, and by a large margin. The other countries are clustered in terms of their saving rates, with the United States and the United Kingdom at the low end of the spectrum.

Chart 2-2. Gross National Saving Rates of Major Industrial Countries
(In percent of GNP)

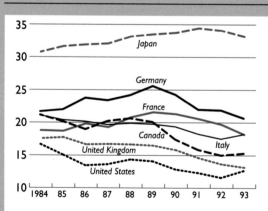

Source: IMF, *World Economic Outlook* (Washington, various issues).

How Much Should Japan Save?

The preceding indicates that Japan's saving rate is high, both in absolute terms and relative to other countries. In saving, a country chooses to forgo current consumption in order to increase future consumption opportunities. Clearly, a balance must be struck between the costs of forgoing consumption today and the benefits of increased future consumption. Too little saving will be suboptimal in that a low level of capital formation will result in a low level of sustainable consumption. Too much saving, however, can also be suboptimal because present and future consumption opportunities are forgone in favor of building and maintaining the stock of capital.[1] Neoclassical growth theory provides at least three separate, but interrelated, conditions by which to assess whether an appropriate balance between consumption and saving (investment) is struck—that is, whether a country is saving too much or too little.[2] These are (1) the (modified) "golden-rule" criterion; (2) the dynamic

---

[1] In such a circumstance, a society puts itself on a path toward capital saturation or overaccumulation, thereby driving the marginal product of capital toward zero.

[2] In a neoclassical growth model, the economy converges to a steady-state balanced-growth path (with a constant capital-labor ratio, constant net rate of return to capital, and a constant rate of growth). The constant long-run rate of growth will equal the (exogenous) rate of population growth plus the (exogenous) pace of technological progress. Although the long-run rate of growth is not affected by the economy's saving rate, the saving rate determines the steady-state capital-labor ratio as well as the level of consumption per capita. Thus, the "choice" of the saving rate has important implications for steady-state consumption opportunities. See Solow (1956), Hahn and Matthews (1964), Jones (1976), and Phelps (1961 and 1966) for an overview of neoclassical growth models and golden rules. Also, see Evans (1992) for a discussion of the neoclassical growth model and the adequacy of saving in the United States.

efficiency condition; and (3) the marginal productivity approach.

Briefly, the golden-rule criterion allows an optimal saving rate to be calculated. If the actual saving rate is less than (greater than) the golden-rule saving rate, then a country is saving too little (too much) from the perspective of maximizing the level of sustainable consumption. In practice, the actual saving rate can be compared with a range of golden-rule saving rates, derived by varying the values of the key parameters (given uncertainties surrounding their exact values). The second condition, the dynamic efficiency criterion, compares profits with investment. So long as profits exceed investment, then capital (the sum of past saving decisions) has not been overaccumulated. The criterion is a variant of the commonly cited proposition that, at the golden rule, all profits are saved (that is, invested). The third criterion, the marginal productivity approach, suggests that capital has not been overaccumulated so long as the net marginal product of capital exceeds the growth rate of the economy or a relevant social discount rate. It is a variant of another commonly cited result of neoclassical growth theory: at the golden rule, the net marginal product of capital is equal to the steady-state growth rate.

"Golden Rule" of Accumulation

In neoclassical growth models, a commonly cited criterion for choosing among saving rates is the golden rule, which maximizes per capita consumption through time. The golden-rule criterion suggests that the highest sustainable level of per capita consumption is attained when the net rate of return on capital equals the sum of the population growth rate and the rate of technological progress. If allowance is made for time preference, then a modified golden-rule proposition emerges under which the welfare-maximizing steady-state path is characterized by the condition that the rate of return on capital minus the rate of pure time preference equals the sum of the population growth rate and the rate of technological progress. In the steady state, a saving rate above or below this welfare-maximizing rate will be suboptimal.[3]

The modified golden rule allows one to calculate the saving rate and the capital-output ratio that would be approached in the long run. Briefly, it can be shown that only two equations need to be parameterized to solve for the optimal steady-state capital-output ratio and saving rate:

$$K/Y = \alpha/(\delta + p + g + n) \qquad (2\text{-}1)$$

$$S/Y = (n + g + \delta)K/Y = \\ \alpha[(n + g + \delta)/(p + n + g + \delta)], \quad (2\text{-}2)$$

where K, Y, S, α, δ, p, g, and n are the capital stock, output, saving, capital's share of output, rate of depreciation, social rate of time preference, exogenous rate of technical progress, and growth rate of the labor force, respectively.[4] Equation (2-1) defines the capital-output ratio consistent with the modified golden rule, and equation (2-2) defines the steady-state saving ratio. From equation (2-2), it is easy to see that if the pure rate of time preference (p) is zero, then the optimal steady-state saving rate is equal to capital's share of output (α)— commonly interpreted in the literature as the proposition that, in the golden-rule steady state, all profits are saved (invested).

Parameter Values

To make the two equations above operational, it is necessary to evaluate the likely values of the parameters in the case of Japan.

Capital's Share of Output (α). National accounts data in Japan suggest that capital's share of national income is about 35 percent. Estimates based on an aggregate production function approach, however, indicate an even higher share (of about 40 percent).[5] For analytical purposes, the work that follows will consider values of 0.35 and 0.40.

Rate of Depreciation (δ). Rates of economic depreciation of 7 percent (low) and 9 percent (high) are considered. This range is based on the recent shift toward relatively shorter-lived assets (in part owing to increasing speeds of technological obsolescence) and takes into account the behavior of the capital goods deflator and the composition of investment (public, private fixed, and residential).

Rate of Technical Progress (g). Assuming that most "catch-up" effects have already occurred, the prospective exogenous rate of technical progress (multifactor productivity growth) is assumed to be about 1 percent a year.[6]

---

[3] Note that, in the short run, a saving rate even higher than the long-run value implied by equation (2-2) below can be justified. This would be the case if the economy were approaching the steady state from below (that is, from a capital-output ratio lower than the long-run capital output). In such an instance, saving might be higher than the long-run rate in response to a rate of return on capital greater than the long-run rate. Saving would eventually fall to its long-run level as the marginal productivity of capital was driven to its long-run rate. In this regard, Christiano (1989) argued that trends in Japan's saving behavior have been associated with efforts to rebuild the capital stock (and the attendant high rates of return to capital) after World War II.

[4] See Evans (1992) for a full description of the methodology and a derivation of the conditions. This section draws heavily from this source.

[5] See, for example, estimates of the aggregate production function in Japan (1993).

[6] Alexander (1994) has noted that, for many sectors of the Japanese economy, significant productivity gaps exist between Japan and the United States, suggesting that either technological catch-up is not as yet complete (or that further capital deepening is necessary). An assumption of slightly higher multifactor productivity growth, however, has a minimal effect on the golden-rule saving rates calculated below, all other things held constant.

Table 2-2. Optimal Gross Saving Rates Under Alternative Parameter Values[1]

Capital Share[2]	Rate of Technical Progress[2]	Gross Saving Rate[2]	Capital-Output Ratio
		$\delta = 7$	
35	0.5	35	4.4
	1.0	35	4.1
		$\delta = 9$	
	0.5	35	3.5
	1.0	35	3.3
		$\delta = 7$	
40	0.5	40	5.0
	1.0	40	4.7
		$\delta = 9$	
	0.5	40	4.0
	1.0	40	3.8

Source: IMF staff calculations.

[1]The calculations assume a labor force growth rate of $\frac{1}{2}$ of 1 percent annually and a social rate of time preference of 0 percent.

[2]In percent.

This value is consistent with the multifactor productivity growth rate embodied in estimates for potential output growth. A lower-bound value of 0.5 percent is also considered.

Growth Rate of the Labor Force (n). Although demographic projections for the total population and for the prime working-age group (aged 15–64) suggest very little growth, a modest rise in the labor force participation rate (especially for women, but also reflecting a gradual boost in the retirement age) is expected. Accordingly, a long-run rate of labor force growth of $\frac{1}{2}$ of 1 percent is utilized.

A final issue that must be considered is the social rate of time preference.[7] Unfortunately, the social rate of time preference is not an observable variable. Rather than assigning an arbitrary value, the approach adopted in this section is to provide a benchmark optimal saving rate and capital-output ratio on the assumption that the social rate of time preference is zero. The revealed social rate of time preference can then be deduced from the deviations of the actual from the optimal rate of saving.[8]

Implied and Actual Saving Rates

Table 2-2 provides illustrative calculations for the optimal saving rates and capital-output ratios implied by the ranges of parameter values outlined above. As can be seen, the golden-rule saving rates are 35 percent and 40 percent (equal, of course, to the assumed capital shares). The long-run capital-output ratios range between 3.3 and 5.0. These results provide a benchmark by which to judge the optimality of recent Japanese saving behavior. During the 1984–93 period, the gross national saving rate in Japan averaged 33 percent of GNP, with a high of 34 percent in 1991 and a low of 31 percent in 1984. In the same period, the capital-output ratio averaged 2.9, with a period-ending high of 3.2.[9]

These figures suggest that Japan's saving rate and capital-output ratio are currently both lower than the long-run steady-state rates implied by a modified golden

---

[7] The social rate of time preference is intended to reflect a society's evaluation of the relative desirability of consumption at different points in time. There is an extensive literature on the choice of the appropriate social rate of time preference, but the little agreement that has emerged suggests that the social rate of time preference is low, if not zero. See Jones (1976, Chapter 9) for a brief summary of the academic debate; see also Sen (1967) and Arrow and Lind (1970) for specific approaches to the issue.

[8] The subsection on dynamic efficiency, below, provides an approach to the question of oversaving that is independent of the social rate of time preference.

[9] Capital-output ratios are derived by cumulating real net investment flows (public, private fixed, residential, and inventory investment) and dividing by real GNP.

rule under a range of reasonable parameter values. On this basis, Japan cannot be said to be oversaving. Indeed, the calculations suggest that Japan could increase its sustainable level of consumption by raising its saving rate by 2 percent of GNP, if capital's share is 35 percent, and by 7 percent of GNP, if capital's share is 40 percent. Note, however, that the deviation between actual and optimal saving rates would be consistent with a nonzero social rate of time preference. The deviation suggests that, with a capital share of 35 percent and allowing the other parameters to take on their range of values, the revealed social rate of time preference is about $\frac{1}{2}$ of 1 percent. If the capital share is 40 percent (and, again, allowing the other parameters to take on their range of values), then the revealed social rate of time preference is 2 percent.

Dynamic Efficiency

An alternative approach to the question of saving behavior that is also derived from neoclassical growth models is the dynamic efficiency criterion. This criterion allows a judgment of whether an economy has overaccumulated capital—that is, oversaved—on the basis of easily observable economic variables. Moreover, while one is left, under the modified golden rule, with a plausible range of saving rates that can be deemed optimal, the dynamic efficiency criterion is a one-way test: it allows one to assess whether the current capital stock is too high—and thus, whether overaccumulation (oversaving) has occurred.

Conceptual Underpinnings

According to the literature on optimal economic growth, an economy is said to be dynamically efficient if it invests less than the return to capital. In the case of dynamic efficiency, the economy has not overaccumulated capital in the sense that the marginal product of capital exceeds the rate of growth of the economy. In the case of dynamic inefficiency, the reverse is true—implying that a "society would be reducing its consumption merely to support the growth of a capital stock which is so large that diminishing returns have robbed it of its capacity to support its own growth and leave a surplus for extra consumption" (Solow (1970, p. 28)). Thus, in a dynamically inefficient economy, it is possible for society to go on a consumption binge, thereby reducing the stock of (overaccumulated) capital. Thereafter, consumption per capita could be higher because resources do not have to be devoted to maintaining an inefficiently large capital stock.

More formally, the condition for an economy to be dynamically efficient can be derived from the steady-state relationship among consumption (C), output (Y), the capital stock (K), and the rate of economic growth (μ):

$$C = Y - \mu K. \qquad (2\text{-}3)$$

Equation (2-3) says that steady-state consumption is equal to steady-state output, less the proportion of output that must be invested each period for the capital stock to grow at the same rate as output.[10] Differentiating equation (2-3) with respect to the capital stock gives

$$dC/dK = dY/dK - \mu = MPK - \mu. \qquad (2\text{-}4)$$

Equation (2-4) implies that steady-state consumption can be raised by increasing the capital stock as long as the marginal product of capital (MPK) exceeds the rate of economic growth. If this is the case, the economy is said to be dynamically efficient: it has not overaccumulated capital. But if the marginal product of capital is less than the rate of economic growth, more capital must be reinvested to maintain a constant capital-output ratio than capital produces at the margin. Consumption is thus reduced to maintain the capital stock at an inefficiently high level.[11]

A final step is needed to implement a test for dynamic efficiency. Multiplying both sides of equation (2-4) by the capital stock results in the following measurable condition for testing whether an economy is in the dynamically efficient region:

$$MPK(K) - \mu(K) = MPK(K) - I \geq 0. \qquad (2\text{-}5)$$

That is, an economy is dynamically efficient if the return to capital exceeds investment.[12] The intuition behind this result is straightforward: if the return to all past investments exceeds current investment, then part of the return is being consumed by society. The capital sector is contributing to consumption opportunities. If this were not the case, then society would never partake in the fruits of earlier sacrifices and would perpetually not only reinvest all the returns from past investment, but also depress current consumption to further add to the capital stock: the capital sector is a drain on consumption opportunities.

Previous Findings

Abel, Mankiw, Summers, and Zeckhauser (1989; hereafter, AMSZ) used equation (2-5) to test for dynamic efficiency in a cross section of countries, including Japan. In their approach, they showed that equation (2-5) holds if production technology exhibits constant returns to scale

---

[10] If the capital stock grows at a rate other than μ, the capital-output ratio would be changing, thus violating the steady-state assumption. For simplicity, depreciation is ignored. It is, however, straightforward to generalize equation (2-3) by adding the depreciation rate to μ.

[11] The golden-rule growth path is defined as the point where $dC/dK = 0$, or where the marginal product of capital equals the rate of economic growth. At this point, the associated capital-output ratio maximizes sustainable consumption. Such a point is consistent with an assumption of a zero rate of social time preference.

[12] Phelps (1966) noted that, in a world of uncertainty, overaccumulation may be optimal, so that a reserve of capital could be consumed in the event of an earthquake, war, or other probabilistic phenomena. In this sense, a strict nonnegativity criterion might not be the appropriate test of dynamic efficiency.

and there are no monopoly profits, so that capital earns a competitive return. Equation (2-5) also requires that a steady state has been achieved. As a result, less weight can and should be given to results pertaining to any individual year; rather, investment rates and returns to capital should be examined for longer (five-year or ten-year) periods (over which it can be assumed that the capital-output ratio is fairly constant). In addition, AMSZ noted that their analysis takes no account of investment in human capital and may be misleading in its treatment of the return to land.[13] Finally, AMSZ ignored the role of public investment in assessing dynamic efficiency (see below).

In examining Japan for the period 1960–84, AMSZ found that the economy is dynamically efficient. The gross profit rate exceeded the investment rate throughout the period by an average of slightly more than 10 percentage points of GNP, although the difference between the rates shows a marked secular decline. In the early 1980s, the average difference falls to about 8¼ percent of GNP, compared with an average difference of 13¾ percentage points in the decade of the 1960s. AMSZ concluded that, despite Japan's high rate of capital accumulation and tradition of low real interest rates, the criterion for dynamic efficiency is comfortably satisfied.

Recent Evidence

The latter part of the 1980s saw a remarkable boom in investment activity, and it is therefore relevant to revisit the question of dynamic efficiency in Japan. The following sections first examine dynamic efficiency along the lines of the AMSZ approach, but extending the results through 1992, and then expand the AMSZ results by considering two other large sources of capital accumulation in Japan: public and foreign investment.

Extending the AMSZ Results

Table 2-3 presents profit and investment rates for the private sector based on national accounts data from Japan's Economic Planning Agency (EPA) for the period 1976–92.[14] Profits are calculated as the sum of operating surpluses of the nonfinancial corporate sector, the finan-

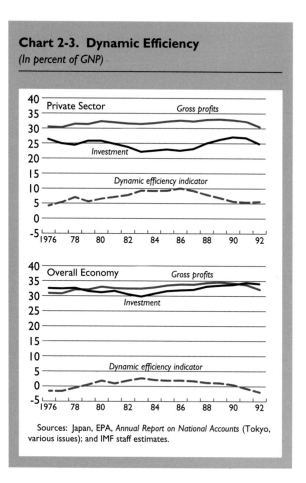

Chart 2-3. Dynamic Efficiency
(In percent of GNP)

Sources: Japan, EPA, *Annual Report on National Accounts* (Tokyo, various issues); and IMF staff estimates.

cial sector, and the unincorporated nonfinancial enterprise sector, plus the capital consumption allowances of these sectors. The operating surplus of the unincorporated nonfinancial enterprise sector has been adjusted downward, since a large part of the operating surplus may actually reflect a return to labor.[15] The adjustment factor used is 65 percent, on the assumption that the return to labor in this sector does not differ significantly from other estimates of labor's share in income. The profit rate is the ratio of gross profits to GNP. The investment rate is the sum of gross fixed capital formation plus inventory accumulation in each of the sectors, relative to GNP.

The data indicate that Japan's private sector has been dynamically efficient over the period (Chart 2-3, top panel). On average, over the 1976–92 period the profit rate exceeded the investment rate by 7.2 percentage points of GNP, with a minimum of 4.2 percent of GNP

---

[13] To take human capital accumulation into account, it is necessary to add investment in human capital to the gross investment figure and to make an estimate of the proportion of wage compensation that is due to human capital formation. This proportion could then be added to the gross profit figure. Although this would be an interesting extension, it is beyond the scope of the present analysis.

For the treatment of land, AMSZ pointed out that part of the gross profit is a return to land, and that as a result the return to capital (the gross profit rate) may be overstated. They noted, however, that research in this area has not produced conclusive results (see AMSZ, p. 9).

[14] AMSZ used data from the Organization for Economic Cooperation and Development (OECD) for their calculations.

---

[15] Because the EPA's national accounts data consolidate the household sector with unincorporated nonfinancial enterprises and include the imputed rent for the flow of services from owner-occupied housing within the (consolidated) operating surplus, this amount is netted for purposes of calculating the wage component of the operating surplus. It is, however, included in the calculation of gross profits.

Table 2-3. Private Sector Dynamic Efficiency

Year	Gross Profits/GNP (1)	Investment/GNP (2)	Dynamic Efficiency Indicator (1) − (2)
1976	30.5	26.3	4.2
1977	30.3	25.0	5.4
1978	31.5	24.4	7.1
1979	31.4	25.8	5.6
1980	32.4	25.8	6.6
1981	32.0	24.8	7.2
1982	31.6	23.8	7.8
1983	31.5	22.2	9.3
1984	31.8	22.6	9.2
1985	32.3	23.0	9.3
1986	32.6	22.6	10.1
1987	32.4	23.1	9.2
1988	32.9	25.0	7.9
1989	33.0	26.2	6.8
1990	32.8	27.1	5.7
1991	32.2	26.8	5.4
1992	30.5	24.9	5.6
Five-year average			
1976–80	31.2	25.5	5.8
1981–85	31.8	23.3	8.6
1986–90	32.7	24.8	7.9
1988–92	32.3	26.0	6.3
Ten-year average			
1976–85	31.5	24.2	7.2
1983–92	32.2	24.4	7.9
Period average			
1976–92	31.9	24.7	7.2

Sources: Japan, Economic Planning Agency (EPA), *Annual Report on National Accounts* (various issues); and IMF staff estimates.

in 1976 and a maximum of 10.1 percent of GNP in 1986. For the decade ending in 1985, the average difference was 7.2 percent of GNP; and for the decade ending in 1992, the average difference was 7.9 percent of GNP.

Role of Public and Foreign Investment

A broader approach to the question of dynamic efficiency is provided by including public as well as foreign investment (saving).[16] Foreign investment (defined as the current account balance less capital transfers) is included because it ultimately represents a claim on capital, even if such claims are not located domestically. Moreover,

such investment (saving), whether located domestically or abroad, represents forgone consumption opportunities, a key issue in deciding whether overaccumulation is occurring. Finally, at a technical level, GNP includes factor incomes from abroad, and thus the return to capital calculated therefrom includes returns to domestic and foreign investment. Government investment is included for two reasons: it is as germane to the question of overaccumulation as private investment; and public investment may well be used by the Government to bring the economy closer to a golden rule. That is, it may well be used to supplement suboptimal private sector investment, brought about by the disincentive effects inherent in government tax and regulatory policies as well as higher than socially optimal rates of time preference in the private sector (see Evans (1992); Foley and Sidrauski (1971); and Atkinson and Sandmo (1980)).

Table 2-4 presents profit and investment rates for this exercise. After public and foreign investment were included, the test indicated that Japan has been dynamically efficient over the period. On average, the profit rate has

---

[16] An alternative test, between the AMSZ approach and the one used here, was also considered: foreign investment (saving) was added to private gross fixed capital formation and inventory accumulation to arrive at a broader measure of private sector accumulation, and net property income from abroad was included in deriving the gross rate of profit—thereby providing an augmented test for private sector dynamic efficiency. The inclusion of these flows does not alter the basic conclusions on private sector dynamic efficiency.

Table 2-4. Aggregate Dynamic Efficiency

Year	Gross Profits/GNP (1)	Investment/GNP (2)	Dynamic Efficiency Indicator (1) − (2)
1976	30.9	32.5	−1.6
1977	30.8	32.4	−1.6
1978	32.1	32.6	−0.5
1979	32.1	31.6	0.6
1980	33.0	31.2	1.9
1981	32.6	31.7	0.9
1982	32.5	30.6	1.9
1983	32.4	29.8	2.7
1984	32.8	30.8	2.1
1985	33.5	31.6	1.9
1986	33.8	31.9	1.9
1987	33.8	32.1	1.7
1988	34.3	33.2	1.2
1989	34.6	33.5	1.1
1990	34.2	33.7	0.5
1991	33.7	34.4	−0.7
1992	32.2	34.1	−1.9
Five-year average			
1976–80	31.8	32.1	−0.3
1981–85	32.8	30.9	1.9
1986–90	34.2	32.9	1.3
1988–92	33.8	33.8	0.0
Ten-year average			
1976–85	32.3	31.5	0.8
1983–92	33.5	32.5	1.1
Period average			
1976–92	32.9	32.2	0.7

Sources: Japan, EPA, *Annual Report on National Accounts* (various issues); and IMF staff estimates.

exceeded the investment rate by 0.7 percentage points of GNP over the 1976–92 period. For the decade ending in 1985, the average difference was 0.8 percent of GNP; and for the decade ending in 1992, the average difference was 1.1 percent of GNP.

In examining the results, two features are apparent. First, the average difference, whether for the entire period or for the identified decades, is positive but small.[17] Second, for some years of the period under investigation, the difference between the gross profit rate and the investment rate is negative. One possible interpretation of these features is that Japan, while dynamically efficient, may be close to an inefficient region. There are, however, a number of reasons, related in part to data and measurement issues, for questioning this interpretation.

Although the average difference between the gross profit rate and the investment rate is relatively small, it is probably substantially understated. The inclusion of public investment, which averaged 8 percent of GNP over the 1976–92 period, results in a bias toward dynamic inefficiency because national accounts data do not make an imputation for the flow of services yielded by the public capital stock, and hence the overall gross profit rate in the economy may well be understated.[18] Moreover,

---

[17] In a policy sense, the size of the difference between the gross profit and investment rates is less germane when the difference is small. It is more relevant when the difference is large, since this may suggest that, although the economy is efficient in that it is not overaccumulating, it does not rule out that the economy may be underaccumulating.

[18] Of course, part of the flow of services may indeed be captured, to the extent that public services are priced (toll roads, airport taxes) or to the extent that the flow of unpriced or underpriced services are captured in firms' profitability or workers' wages. The degree of complementarity among public capital, private capital, and labor inputs then becomes an issue. Still, to the extent that a large part of the service flow from public investment is not captured and imputed, the difference between gross profit and investment may be significantly biased downward—that is, away from dynamic efficiency.

the period under investigation includes subperiods of two major recessions (1976–78, when the economy was still in a recovery phase from the first oil shock; and 1991–92, the onset of the current recession). In general, cyclical conditions can adversely affect measures of dynamic efficiency—both because gross profits tend to fall and because declines in private investment may well be compensated by increases in countercyclical public investment expenditure measures. This consideration is particularly relevant for the two subperiods in which the difference between the gross profit rates and investment rates are negative. Finally, as noted earlier, because of the underlying steady-state assumption, that the measure of dynamic efficiency in any one year shows a negative difference cannot be taken as conclusive evidence of inefficiency. Rather, averages over longer periods are more germane. That cyclical conditions also influence the measure of dynamic efficiency bolsters the argument for looking at averages over five- or ten-year periods.

In summary, the results indicate that Japan is dynamically efficient; that is, it has not overaccumulated capital. This is true whether narrow (private sector) or broader concepts (including government capital and foreign investment) of accumulation are considered.

Marginal Productivity

A third approach to the question of over- or undersaving involves calculating the marginal productivity of capital, and comparing it either with a measure of the opportunity cost of savings or with the growth rate of the economy. The former comparison is really a cost-benefit approach (or deadweight loss approach),[19] wherein a demand price (or marginal social benefit) is compared with a supply price (or opportunity cost variable). The latter comparison is related both to the golden rule and to dynamic efficiency.

Cost-Benefit Approach

The cost-benefit approach is a direct test of whether an economy is oversaving or not. If the marginal product of capital exceeds the opportunity cost of saving, then an incremental unit of saving will increase intertemporal consumption opportunities. The problem then becomes one of estimating the marginal product of capital and finding a measure of the opportunity cost of saving.

The marginal product of capital can be computed from national accounts data and a measure of the capital-output ratio. Assuming that aggregate output is governed by a Cobb-Douglas production function with constant returns

to scale, gross profits as a share of output are equal to capital's share of output:

$$(gross\ profits/Y) = \alpha$$
$$= [f'(k)(K)]/Y = r(K/Y). \qquad (2\text{-}6)$$

Dividing equation (2-6) by the capital-output ratio yields the marginal product of capital, r:

$$(gross\ profits/Y)/(K/Y) = \alpha/(K/Y)$$
$$= f'(k) = r. \qquad (2\text{-}7)$$

In turn, subtracting depreciation yields a net return to capital:

$$R = r - \delta. \qquad (2\text{-}8)$$

This (net-of-depreciation) return can be compared with a variable for the opportunity cost of saving.

As regards the opportunity cost of saving, various authors have considered alternative approaches. Some (for example, Harberger (1972) and Feldstein (1977)) adjusted the return to capital for corporate and personal taxes to find the net-of-tax return received by investors.[20] The supply price of saving derived from this exercise is the market's revelation of investors' rate of time discount. Although such an approach is useful in measuring the deadweight loss associated with capital market distortions, it is less useful in addressing the issue of oversaving—since, by construction, the demand price will exceed the supply price. Others (for example, Feldstein (1977) and Boskin (1986)) have used cardinalist utility approaches to derive a theoretical supply price. Under these approaches, assumptions about the elasticity of marginal utility with respect to consumption and the marginal rate of substitution between consumption at different dates are made to derive a "planner's" rate of time preference, which is a function of the rate of consumption growth. The planner's rate of time preference can in turn be augmented to take into account individuals' myopia and the probability of death in order to find the private rate of time preference. Either of these rates, depending on the situation, can then be compared with the return to capital to establish whether too much or too little saving is taking place.

The approach taken here is along lines of the latter approach: thus, so long as the calculated return to capital is greater than a range of values for the "planner's" or social rate of time preference, oversaving cannot be said to have occurred. Table 2-5 presents data for alternative measures of the return to capital under alternative depreciation rates of 7 percent and 9 percent. The first measure is an estimate of the return to private capital; the second is the return to private and public capital. Again, because of cyclical and other influences, both annual and period averages are provided.

---

[19] That is, to the extent that the demand price differs from the supply price, the deadweight loss of the distortion (as well as the theoretical level of saving and investment in an undistorted market) can be calculated on the basis of estimated values for the interest elasticities of saving and investment.

[20] Alternatively, the average net-of-tax return to savers can be compared directly with the net return to capital, attributing the difference to a tax wedge.

Table 2-5. Return to Capital

Year	Private Sector Return to Capital		Aggregate Economy Return to Capital		Growth Rate of Real GNP
	$\delta = 7$	$\delta = 9$	$\delta = 7$	$\delta = 9$	
1976	10.7	8.7	5.3	3.3	4.2
1977	10.4	8.4	5.0	3.0	4.8
1978	11.0	9.0	5.4	3.4	5.0
1979	10.9	8.9	5.3	3.3	5.6
1980	11.1	9.1	5.3	3.3	3.5
1981	10.6	8.6	4.9	2.9	3.4
1982	10.2	8.2	4.7	2.7	3.4
1983	10.0	8.0	4.5	2.5	2.8
1984	10.2	8.2	4.7	2.7	4.3
1985	10.6	8.6	5.0	3.0	5.2
1986	10.4	8.4	5.0	3.0	2.6
1987	10.1	8.1	4.9	2.9	4.3
1988	10.5	8.5	5.2	3.2	6.2
1989	10.2	8.2	5.2	3.2	4.8
1990	9.6	7.6	4.9	2.9	4.8
1991	8.9	6.9	4.6	2.6	4.3
1992	7.4	5.4	3.6	1.6	1.4
Five-year average					
1976–80	10.8	8.8	5.2	3.2	4.6
1981–85	10.3	8.3	4.8	2.8	3.8
1986–90	10.2	8.2	5.1	3.1	4.6
1988–92	9.3	7.3	4.7	2.7	4.3
Ten-year average					
1976–85	10.6	8.6	5.0	3.0	4.2
1983–92	9.8	7.8	4.8	2.8	4.1
Period average					
1976–92	10.2	8.2	4.9	2.9	4.2

Sources: Japan, EPA, *Annual Report on National Accounts* (various issues); and IMF staff estimates.

As can be seen, the first measure averages 10 percent over the full period at the depreciation rate of 7 percent. If the higher rate of depreciation is used, the average is 8 percent. Thus, for values of the social rate of discount as high as even 2 percent, the data suggest that capital accumulation in Japan has not driven the stock of capital to the point that the return to capital is below the relevant opportunity cost. The second measure, although smaller, also exceeds reasonable values of the social rate of time preference. Again, recall that this measure may be biased downward because the national accounts make no imputation for the flow of services from the government capital stock. Indeed, all the caveats discussed in the section on dynamic efficiency apply equally to this measure.

Growth Rate Approach

The return to capital can also be compared with the real rate of economic growth, reflecting the standard result from growth theory that, at the golden rule, $R = g$.[21] Thus, if $R > g$, then the capital stock has not reached its golden-rule level, and the economy cannot be said to have overaccumulated.[22] For this reason, Table 2-5 also includes a column on the real rate of economic growth. The private sector return to capital exceeds the real rate of economic growth for both of the assumed rates of

---

[21] This can easily be seen in the derivation for the dynamic efficiency criteria above.

[22] Note that a number of authors have compared the growth rate with the risk-free real interest rate, rather than with the net return to capital. In general they have found that the real risk-free rate is lower than the real growth rate, which would in turn suggest that capital overaccumulation has occurred. Other authors, however, note that the return on equities has substantially exceeded the real growth rate of the economy and that the test for capital overaccumulation based solely on the risk-free rate of return may not be sufficiently rigorous (see, for example, Blanchard and Fischer (1989) and Boskin (1986)).

depreciation. For the aggregate economy, the return to capital exceeds the growth rate of the economy at a depreciation rate of 7 percent, but it is lower than the growth rate of the economy at a depreciation rate of 9 percent. Once again, the same caveats apply. Using a modified golden-rule result does not alter these findings for reasonable values of the social rate of time preference.[23] In sum, comparing rates of return with growth rates of the economy suggests that the golden-rule level of capital stock is unlikely to have been exceeded.

Conclusions

This section has used conditions from neoclassical growth theory to investigate Japanese saving behavior. More specifically, three separate but interrelated tests were conducted to determine whether the flow of saving or the stock of accumulated capital could be deemed "excessive" from an economic viewpoint. The modified golden-rule criteria, although perhaps the weakest of the three tests (because of the uncertainty surrounding parameter values), suggests that Japan's recent saving behavior and capital-output ratio are lower than those consistent with maximizing the level of sustainable consumption over the long run. Tests of dynamic efficiency indicated that for the period 1975–92 Japan has not overaccumulated capital. The result holds for both the private sector as well as the aggregate economy (that is, including public and foreign investment). A final test relating to the marginal productivity of capital showed that the net rates of return to capital have generally exceeded opportunity costs, unless the depreciation rate is assumed to be relatively high. Again, this was true both for the private sector and for the aggregate economy.

Still, it is important to recognize several caveats with respect to the work that has been presented. First, as regards the golden-rule approach, there is some uncertainty about the relevant parameter values. In addition, the social rate of time preference is an unobservable variable. Second, there may be a bias introduced in the tests for dynamic efficiency as well as those for the marginal productivity because national accounts data do not make an imputation for the service flows generated by public investment. Finally, to the extent that Japan is still in the process of capital deepening, technological catch-up, or even postwar reconstruction, the assumption that the economy is at or near a steady state may not be justified. Notwithstanding these caveats, the three sets of tests, whether looked at individually or together, suggest that neither Japan's flow of saving nor its stock of accumulated capital can be considered excessive from the perspective of maximizing sustainable consumption.

---

[23] Under a modified golden rule, if the rate of return to capital less the rate of time preference exceeds the growth rate of the economy, then the economy cannot be said to have overaccumulated.

References

Abel, Andrew B., Gregory N. Mankiw, Lawrence H. Summers, and Richard J. Zeckhauser, "Assessing Dynamic Efficiency: Theory and Evidence," *Review of Economic Studies*, Vol. 56 (January 1989), pp. 1–20.

Aghevli, Bijan, and others, *The Role of National Saving in the World Economy: Recent Trends and Prospects*, IMF Occasional Paper 67 (Washington: International Monetary Fund, 1990).

Alexander, Arthur J., "Japan as Number Three: Long-Term Productivity and Growth Problems in the Economy," Report 17a (Washington: Japan Economic Institute, April 29, 1994).

Arrow, Kenneth, and Robert Lind, "Uncertainty and the Evaluation of Public Investment Decisions," *American Economic Review*, Vol. 60 (June 1970), pp. 364–78.

Atkinson, A.B., and A. Sandmo, "Welfare Implications of the Taxation of Savings," *Economic Journal*, Vol. 90 (September 1980), pp. 529–49.

Blanchard, Olivier Jean, and Stanley Fischer, *Lectures on Macroeconomics* (Cambridge, Massachusetts: MIT Press, 1989).

Boskin, Michael, "Theoretical and Empirical Issues in the Measurement, Evaluation, and Interpretation of Postwar U.S. Saving," in *Savings and Capital Formation: The Policy Options*, edited by F. Gerard Adams and Susan M. Wachter (Lexington, Massachusetts: Lexington Books, 1986).

Cass, D., "Optimum Growth in an Aggregative Model of Capital Accumulation," *Review of Economic Studies*, Vol. 32 (1965), pp. 233–40.

———, "On Capital Overaccumulation in the Aggregative Neoclassical Model of Economic Growth: A Complete Characterization," *Journal of Economic Theory*, Vol. 4 (1972), pp. 200–23.

Christiano, Lawrence J., "Understanding Japan's Saving Rate: The Reconstruction Hypothesis," *Federal Reserve Bank of Minneapolis Quarterly Review*, Vol. 13 (Spring 1989).

Evans, Owen, "National Savings and Targets for the Federal Budget Balance," in *The United States Economy: Performance and Issues*, edited by Y. Horiguchi and others (Washington: International Monetary Fund, 1992).

Feldstein, Martin, "Does the United States Save Too Little?" *American Economic Review*, Vol. 67 (February 1977), pp. 116–21.

Foley, Duncan K., and Miguel Sidrauski, *Monetary and Fiscal Policy in a Growing Economy* (London: Macmillan, 1971).

Hahn, F.H., and R.C.O. Matthews, "The Theory of Economic Growth," *Economic Journal*, Vol. 64 (December 1964), pp. 779–902.

Harberger, Arnold C., *Project Evaluation: Collected Papers* (New York: Macmillan, 1972; Chicago: University of Chicago Press, 1976).

Japan, Economic Planning Agency (EPA), *Economic Survey of Japan, 1992–1993* (Tokyo, July 1993).

Jones, Hywel G., *An Introduction to Modern Theories of Economic Growth* (New York: McGraw-Hill, 1976).

Phelps, Edmund. S., "The Golden Rule of Accumulation: A Fable for Growthmen," *American Economic Review*, Vol. 51 (1961), pp. 638–43.

_____, *Golden Rules of Economic Growth: Studies of Efficient and Optimal Investment* (New York: Norton, 1966).

Sen, A.K., "Isolation, Assurance, and the Social Rate of Discount," *Quarterly Journal of Economics*, February 1967, pp. 112–24.

Solow, Robert, "A Contribution to the Theory of Economic Growth," *Quarterly Journal of Economics*, Vol. 32 (1956), pp. 65–94.

_____, "Comment on the Golden Rule," *Review of Economic Studies*, Vol. 29 (June 1962), pp. 255–57.

_____, *Growth Theory: An Exposition*, (Oxford: Clarendon, 1970).

III Japan's Capital Flows

Juha Kähkönen

Since the early 1980s, Japan has been the world's largest exporter of capital. Despite having the highest investment rate of all major industrial countries, Japan has invested less at home than it has saved, transferring part of its saving abroad and, as a consequence, running current account surpluses. From modest amounts in 1980, outflows of portfolio capital and foreign direct investment (FDI) have since surged; Japan has also become the world's largest provider of development assistance. This section discusses the developments in Japan's net capital outflows, with particular attention paid to the determinants and impact of Japan's FDI.

The first part provides an overview of capital flows and Japan's international asset position since 1980. Three phases can be distinguished. In the first half of the 1980s, Japan's long-term capital outflows, especially portfolio investment, grew rapidly in line with the current account surplus, helped by the liberalization of capital controls. During the second half, the rise in net long-term outflows accelerated, with direct investment gaining importance, but these outflows were partially offset by large net borrowing of short-term capital. These developments were driven by deregulation of domestic financial markets, further capital account liberalization, rising domestic asset prices, and a sharp appreciation of the yen. So far in the 1990s, net long-term outflows have been well below the level reached in the latter half of the 1980s, and Japan's rising current account surpluses have been accompanied by reductions in short-term liabilities. The changed pattern of Japan's capital flows reflects the completion of the stock adjustment following relaxation of capital controls, the collapse of the asset price "bubble," and banks' response to the introduction of Bank of International Settlements (BIS) capital adequacy guidelines.

The second part of the section focuses on FDI. Japan's outward FDI gained high visibility in the second half of the 1980s, with Japan becoming the largest investor in the world (in flow terms) and with the stock of overseas investment growing fivefold between 1985 and 1992. The pattern of Japanese FDI also changed, from resource-oriented investment in developing countries toward the acquisition of real estate and financial institutions in the major industrial countries. Although much of Japan's FDI can be seen as part of a process of evolving comparative advantage, the same macroeconomic factors that pro-

vided incentives for other types of long-term capital outflows (such as the yen appreciation, the extraordinary rise in asset prices, and liberalization of foreign exchange controls) were also important determinants of the surge in Japan's FDI in the late 1980s. The rise in Japan's FDI can be seen as beneficial to the world economy; not only has it provided potential for the usual gains from international integration to be realized, but there are, in addition, possible positive spillovers into the host economies in the form of new technology and organizational skills. Although FDI, like domestic investment, has effects on the structure of output and employment, any permanent impact on total employment is likely to be small. Similarly, because FDI is unlikely to have a significant influence on the underlying determinants of saving and investment, Japanese FDI will probably have only temporary effects on the current account position.

Recent Developments in the Capital Account

Japan's capital flows have been the counterpart of the current account balance (Chart 3-1). The current account surplus rose rapidly until 1986–87, reaching a peak of 4¼ percent of GDP in 1986. (In U.S. dollars, the peak came in 1987, at $87 billion.) Thereafter, the surplus declined steadily, to a low of 1¼ percent of GDP ($36 billion) in 1990. In the early 1990s, the surplus again rose sharply, stabilizing at about 3 percent of GDP in 1992–93. (In U.S. dollars, an all-time high of $131 billion was recorded in 1993.)

In most years, the combined net outflow of short-term and long-term capital closely matched the current account surplus (Table 3-1). The exceptions were the years 1986–88 and 1993, when a significant part of the surplus was channeled to official reserves, owing to intervention by the Bank of Japan in the foreign exchange market. In particular, in 1987 the monetary authorities absorbed about one half of the current account surplus.

Developments in Japan's capital account since 1980 can be divided into three markedly different phases. In the first half of the decade, long-term capital flows (gross and net) grew rapidly, albeit from a low base, while

Chart 3-1. Current Account Balance and Capital Flows

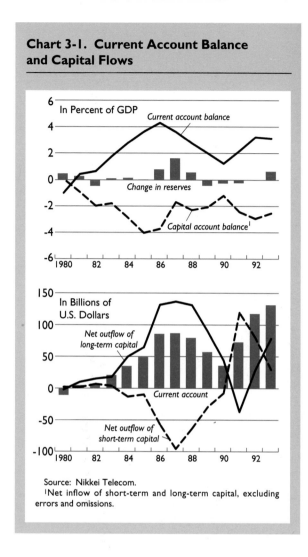

Source: Nikkei Telecom.
[1]Net inflow of short-term and long-term capital, excluding errors and omissions.

Chart 3-2. Foreign Assets and Liabilities

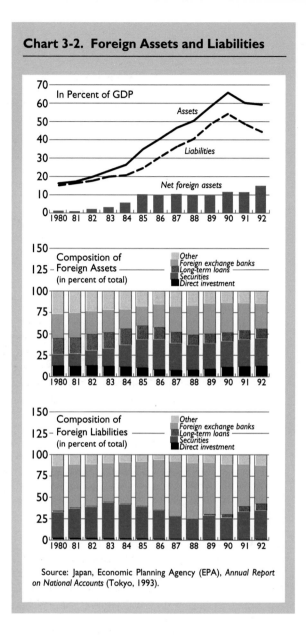

Source: Japan, Economic Planning Agency (EPA), *Annual Report on National Accounts* (Tokyo, 1993).

short-term flows were relatively small and stable, owing to limits on banks' open short positions in foreign currencies. Overall, Japan's net foreign assets rose from 1 percent of GDP in 1980 to 6 percent of GDP in 1984 (Chart 3-2). The buoyancy of long-term flows was largely the result of the liberalization of capital controls, starting with the revision of the Foreign Exchange and Transactions Control Law in December 1980, which, among other things, abolished the system of prior approval for foreign securities investment. As a result, both the flow of portfolio capital and the share of securities in foreign assets and liabilities increased markedly during the period. An extensive system of monitoring and administrative guidance remained in place, however, and ceilings on purchases of foreign securities were an effective constraint on an even faster reallocation of Japanese investors' portfolios.

In the second half of the 1980s, gross long-term capital outflows continued their rapid rise, with foreign direct investment becoming an important component of capital exports, and net long-term outflow also reached record levels. In contrast to developments earlier in the decade, however, there was a large net inflow of short-term capital. Reflecting these partially offsetting flows, Japan's net foreign asset position remained stable at around 10 percent of GDP in 1985–89. A combination of factors was responsible for the pattern of capital flows observed during this period. Dismantling of capital controls again played an important role. This time the liberalization measures not only stimulated long-term capital outflows but also enabled banks to import substantial amounts of short-term capital, since limits on open short positions in

Table 3-1. Summary of the Capital Account
(In billions of U.S. dollars)

	1980	1981	1982	1983	1984	1985	1986	1987	1988	1989	1990	1991	1992	1993
Current account balance	−10.7	4.8	6.8	20.8	35.0	49.2	85.8	87.0	79.6	57.2	35.8	72.9	117.6	131.4
Net long-term capital	2.3	−9.7	−15.0	−17.7	−49.7	−64.5	−131.5	−136.5	−130.9	−89.2	−43.6	37.1	−28.5	−78.3
By type of capital														
Net direct investment	−2.1	−4.7	−4.1	−3.2	−6.0	−5.8	−14.3	−18.4	−34.7	−45.2	−46.3	−29.4	−14.5	−13.6
Net securities	9.4	4.4	2.1	−1.9	−23.6	−43.0	−101.4	−93.8	−66.7	−28.0	−5.0	41.0	−26.2	−62.7
Bonds	...	...	−1.0	−10.1	−23.3	−49.0	−95.1	−66.2	−107.4	−91.7	−12.0	−47.0	−43.8	−30.1
Equities and other	...	...	3.2	8.3	−0.3	5.9	−6.3	−27.6	40.8	63.6	6.9	87.9	17.6	−32.6
Net loans	−2.8	−5.3	−8.1	−8.5	−12.0	−10.5	−9.3	−16.3	−15.3	−4.7	16.9	25.0	8.3	−3.8
Other	−2.1	−4.1	−4.9	−4.2	−8.1	−5.2	−6.5	−8.0	−14.3	−11.3	−9.2	0.4	3.9	1.9
By asset or liability														
Asset	−10.8	−22.8	−27.4	−32.5	−56.8	−81.8	−132.1	−132.8	−149.9	−192.1	−120.8	−121.4	−58.0	−73.6
Direct investment	−2.4	−4.9	−4.5	−3.6	−6.0	−6.5	−14.5	−19.5	−34.2	−44.1	−48.0	−30.7	−17.2	−13.7
Securities	−3.8	−8.8	−9.7	−16.0	−30.8	−59.8	−102.0	−87.8	−86.9	−113.2	−39.7	−74.3	−34.4	−51.7
Bonds	...	...	−6.1	−12.5	−26.8	−53.5	−93.0	−72.9	−85.8	−94.1	−29.0	−68.2	−35.6	−29.9
Equities and other	...	...	−3.7	−3.5	−4.0	−6.3	−9.0	−14.9	−1.1	−19.1	−10.7	−6.1	1.3	−21.8
Loans	−2.6	−5.1	−7.9	−8.4	−11.9	−10.4	−9.3	−16.2	−15.2	−22.5	−22.2	−13.1	−7.6	−8.2
Other	−2.1	−4.1	−5.2	−4.4	−8.1	−5.2	−6.4	−9.4	−13.5	−12.3	−10.9	−3.3	1.2	−0.1
Liabilities	13.1	13.1	12.4	14.8	7.1	17.3	0.6	−3.7	19.0	102.9	77.2	158.5	29.5	−4.7
Direct investment	0.3	0.2	0.4	0.4	—	0.6	0.2	1.2	−0.5	−1.1	1.8	1.4	2.7	0.1
Securities	13.1	13.2	11.9	14.1	7.2	16.7	0.5	−6.1	20.3	85.1	34.7	115.3	8.2	−11.1
Bonds	...	...	5.0	2.4	3.5	4.5	−2.1	6.7	−21.6	2.4	17.0	21.2	−8.2	−0.2
Equities and other	...	...	6.8	11.8	3.7	12.2	2.7	−12.8	41.9	82.7	17.7	94.0	16.4	−10.9
Loans	−0.2	−0.2	−0.2	—	−0.1	−0.1	—	−0.1	−0.1	17.8	39.1	38.1	15.9	4.3
Other	—	−0.1	0.3	0.2	—	—	−0.1	1.3	−0.8	1.0	1.7	3.7	2.7	1.9
Errors and omissions	−3.1	0.5	4.7	2.1	3.7	4.0	2.5	−3.9	2.8	−22.0	−20.9	−7.8	−10.5	−0.3
Basic balance[1]	−11.5	−4.4	−3.4	5.2	−10.9	−11.4	−43.2	−53.4	−48.5	−54.1	−28.7	102.1	78.6	52.9
Short-term capital	−1.9	−1.3	−6.6	−3.5	13.3	9.9	56.9	95.7	64.0	29.4	7.8	−119.2	−80.0	−29.4
Bank	−5.0	−3.6	−5.0	−3.6	17.6	10.8	58.5	71.8	44.5	8.6	−13.6	−93.5	−73.0	−15.0
Nonbank	3.1	2.3	−1.6	0.0	−4.3	−0.9	−1.6	23.9	19.5	20.8	21.5	−25.8	−7.0	−14.4
Overall balance	−13.4	−5.7	−10.0	1.6	2.4	−1.5	13.7	42.3	15.5	−24.7	−20.9	−17.1	−1.4	23.5
Increase in reserves	4.9	3.2	−5.1	1.2	1.8	0.2	15.7	39.2	16.2	−12.8	−7.8	−8.1	−0.3	26.9
Other[2]	−18.3	−8.9	−4.9	0.4	0.5	−1.7	−2.0	3.0	−0.7	−11.9	−13.0	−9.0	−1.1	−3.5

Source: Bank of Japan, *Balance of Payments Monthly* (Tokyo, various issues).

[1] Including errors and omissions.

[2] Including yen-denominated holdings of foreign monetary authorities (with sign reversed).

foreign currencies were lifted in June 1984.[1] Deregulation and structural changes in the domestic financial sector also had a major impact. Deregulation increased competition and induced domestic financial institutions to search

---

[1] The measures that helped to increase long-term flows included permitting various types of Euroyen transactions, allowing resident purchases of foreign-currency-denominated certificates of deposit and commercial paper (both in 1984), and raising the ceilings on purchases of foreign securities (starting in 1986).

for profit opportunities abroad, while a structural change from depository-type financial institutions (such as postal savings banks) toward securities-oriented institutions (such as insurance companies and investment trusts) increased a trend toward foreign securities holding. The sharp increases in land and equity prices during the bubble period in the late 1980s also contributed to the accumulation of foreign assets by Japanese residents. Rising asset prices made equity-related bond issues a low-cost form of financing, and institutional investors were able to convert capital gains into income gains by engaging in capital account transactions.[2] Finally, the sharp appreciation of the yen, especially in 1985–86, stimulated net capital outflows by providing incentives for FDI.

The 1990s have witnessed a major departure from past patterns of capital flows. The gross outflow of long-term capital has declined dramatically from the record level in 1989, and the net long-term outflow has been subdued (it even was negative in 1991). Further, having borrowed heavily short term in the latter half of the 1980s, Japan has become a major net exporter of short-term capital in the 1990s. These developments are largely the result of three factors. First, the stock adjustment following relaxation of capital controls appears to have been largely completed by the late 1980s, with Japanese investors having had sufficient time to reach a desired degree of international diversification. Consequently, these investors became more sensitive to the fundamental determinants of capital flows, including interest rate differentials (adjusted for expected exchange rate changes) and exchange risk. The already heavy exposure to foreign currency assets, the associated exchange risk, and reduced interest differentials in favor of foreign-currency-denominated assets following the tightening of Japanese monetary policy from mid-1989 all reduced incentives for continued rapid accumulation of foreign assets.

Second, the collapse of the asset price bubble in 1990 reduced financial institutions' "hidden" assets (unrealized capital gains). Because exchange losses could not be offset by capital gains to the same extent as before, the institutions became reluctant to purchase foreign securities. The bursting of the bubble also depressed net capital outflow by attracting foreign buyers of Japanese equity and by discouraging direct investment abroad, especially in real estate. Third, concern about capital adequacy, in particular the need to conform with BIS guidelines, made banks adjust their international strategy. Although banks had in the 1980s accumulated large amounts of long-term foreign assets (closely matched by short-term borrowing in foreign currencies, to satisfy regulations to keep banks' open foreign currency positions within a narrow limit), they now had to downsize their international positions.

Long-Term Capital Flows

Accompanying the increase in the current account surplus up to 1987, net long-term capital outflows rose rapidly, reaching a high of $137 billion in 1987. With the external surplus falling in 1988–90, the deficit in the long-term capital account also narrowed. In 1991, however, when the current account surplus again started to rise, there was a net inflow of long-term capital, of $37 billion, for the first time since 1980. In 1992–93, the long-term capital account again recorded net outflows, but the amounts ($29 billion in 1992 and $78 billion in 1993) were well below the average annual outflow of $110 billion in the second half of the 1980s.

The ups and downs in net outflows of long-term capital were the result of a markedly different pattern of growth in assets (foreign assets accumulated by Japanese residents—outflow) and liabilities (Japanese assets acquired by foreigners—inflow). The outflow grew rapidly throughout the 1980s, peaking at $192 billion (6½ percent of GDP) in 1989, but it declined thereafter and averaged $66 billion in 1992–93 (see Table 3-3). By contrast, the inflow was relatively small—less than $20 billion annually—until 1989, when it jumped to over $100 billion. The inflow peaked in 1991 at $159 billion, which exceeded that year's outflow. In 1992–93, however, the inflow returned to the low pre-1989 levels, averaging $13 billion.

Securities have been by far the most important vehicle for transferring Japan's savings surpluses abroad, accounting for 52 percent of the net outflow in 1980–93. Investment by Japanese residents in foreign securities grew more than tenfold between 1982 and 1986, reaching a high of $113 billion in 1989. The rapid rise in securities investment was almost entirely in the form of bonds (Table 3-2). In the second half of the 1980s, the bulk of this rise was the result of increased offshore intermediation of Japanese funds in the form of purchases by Japanese investors of equity-related bonds issued by Japanese companies in Euromarkets.[3] When a major plunge in stock prices in Tokyo made equity warrants less desirable in 1990, securities investment abroad also declined sharply and has remained subdued, averaging $50 billion annually in 1990–93.

Japanese investment in securities other than regular bonds has generally been small. Purchases of foreign stocks and shares have been relatively limited, exceeding $10 billion only twice (in 1987 and 1989). The small

---

[2] Life insurance companies—major institutional investors—had accumulated a large amount of unrealized capital gains ("hidden" assets) that they could not, according to regulations, distribute to policy holders. However, income gains from foreign securities (which earned higher nominal interest rates than Japanese assets) could be distributed, and capital losses owing to the depreciation of the U.S. dollar could be offset by capital gains from domestic assets—as long as the prices of domestic assets were high and rising. This explains the seemingly puzzling buoyancy of Japanese purchases of foreign securities even when the U.S. dollar was widely expected to depreciate. See Kawai (1991, p. 20) for further discussion.

[3] Many Japanese companies chose to issue dollar-denominated warrants (often combined with currency and interest rate swaps) in the Euromarket to raise funds on favorable terms, avoiding the high cost of flotation in the more restricted Tokyo market. The bulk of these warrants were bought by Japanese institutional investors in the expectation of large capital gains in the then-bullish Tokyo stock market.

Table 3-2. Flows of Securities
(In billions of U.S. dollars)

	1980	1985	1986	1987	1988	1989	1990	1991	1992	1993
Net securities (+ = outflow)	−9.4	43.0	101.4	93.8	66.7	28.0	5.0	−41.0	26.2	−62.7
Japan's investment in										
foreign securities	3.8	59.8	102.0	87.8	86.9	113.2	39.7	74.3	34.4	51.7
Stocks and shares	−0.2	1.0	7.0	16.9	3.0	17.9	6.3	3.6	−3.0	15.3
Bonds	3.0	53.5	93.0	72.9	85.8	94.1	29.0	68.2	35.6	29.9
Yen-denominated external bonds, etc.	1.0	5.3	1.9	−2.0	−1.9	1.2	4.5	2.5	1.7	6.4
Foreign investment in										
Japanese securities	13.1	16.7	0.5	−6.1	20.3	85.1	34.7	115.3	8.2	−11.1
Stocks and shares	6.5	−0.7	−15.8	−42.8	6.8	7.0	−13.3	46.8	8.7	20.0
Bonds	5.3	4.5	−2.1	6.7	−21.6	2.4	17.0	21.2	−8.2	−0.2
External bonds	1.2	12.9	18.4	30.1	35.1	75.7	30.9	47.3	7.6	−30.8

Source: Bank of Japan, *Balance of Payments Monthly* (Tokyo, various issues).

share of foreign stocks in Japanese equity portfolios could reflect that stocks, compared with bonds, are less standardized and more difficult to manage (Kawai (1991)) or that Japanese investors expect higher average returns in the domestic stock market than in foreign stock markets (French and Poterba (1991)).[4] Japanese purchases of Samurai bonds (yen-denominated external bonds) and Shogun bonds (dollar-denominated external bonds issued in Tokyo) have also been small.

FDI, which had averaged $4 billion in the first half of the 1980s, became an increasingly important contributor to the intermediation of the saving surpluses in the latter half of the decade. A peak was reached in 1990, when outward FDI amounted to $48 billion and accounted for 40 percent of the total outflow of long-term capital. Since then, however, FDI has declined steadily, falling to $14 billion in 1993. (For a more detailed discussion of developments in FDI, see "Foreign Direct Investment," below.)

Long-term loans extended by Japanese residents (including official development assistance) were more important than FDI until the mid-1980s, but the situation

has subsequently been reversed. Other outflows, including trade credits, have typically been a very small share of total outflows.

The Japanese long-term capital outflow has been directed mainly to industrial countries (Table 3-3).[5] In 1988–93, the United States and the European Union (EU) received three fourths of the outflow. The newly industrializing Asian economies (Hong Kong, Korea, Singapore, and Taiwan Province of China) were the destination of less than 2 percent of Japan's long-term capital exports. Although about one half of outward FDI went to the United States, over 60 percent of Japanese investment in securities was directed to the EU, in particular Luxembourg and the United Kingdom. Both countries offer Euromarkets where many Japanese firms issued equity-related external bonds. In addition, in London, U.K. "gilts" also attract Japanese investors. Loans have been primarily channeled to developing countries (included in the "other" category in Table 3-3).

Long-term capital inflows have mainly been in the form of securities, which have generally been even more dominant than in the case of outflows (Table 3-4). Purchases of Japanese securities by foreigners were particularly important in 1989, when Japanese residents issued large amounts of overseas bonds, and in 1991, when sharply lower equity prices in Japan led foreign investors to buy a record-high amount of stocks in Tokyo, in addition to continued large purchases of Japanese bonds by nonresidents. With inward foreign investment having

---

[4] French and Poterba (1991) studied the reasons for the tendency of portfolio investors in major industrial countries to hold nearly all of their equity in domestic stocks, despite the well-known benefits of international diversification. (They estimate that Japanese investors had only 1.9 percent of their equity in foreign stocks at end-1989.) After concluding that institutional constraints do not play a major role, French and Poterba showed that current portfolio patterns are consistent with the explanation that investors in each nation expect returns in their domestic equity market to be several hundred basis points higher than returns in other markets.

---

[5] Offshore intermediation of Japanese funds makes it difficult to establish the actual destination of some types of outflows.

Table 3-3. Long-Term Capital Outflow by Region and Type

	Year	Total	Direct Investment	Securities	Loans	Other
			In billions of U.S. dollars			
Total	1988	149.9	34.2	86.9	15.2	13.5
	1989	192.1	44.1	113.2	22.5	12.3
	1990	120.8	48.0	39.7	22.2	10.9
	1991	121.4	30.7	74.3	13.1	3.3
	1992	58.0	17.2	34.4	7.6	−1.2
	1993	73.6	13.7	51.7	8.2	0.1
United States	1988	61.5	19.0	36.2	2.8	3.5
	1989	57.1	21.2	26.7	5.0	4.3
	1990	16.4	25.6	−16.2	3.2	3.8
	1991	35.0	15.2	15.6	2.8	1.5
	1992	22.8	8.9	8.5	4.8	0.6
	1993	33.9	6.8	22.0	5.7	−0.5
European Union	1988	55.5	5.8	42.6	1.8	5.4
	1989	85.5	9.7	67.7	4.7	3.3
	1990	58.0	11.0	39.5	5.2	2.3
	1991	49.5	8.0	41.0	—	0.6
	1992	26.3	3.4	27.4	−3.4	−1.2
	1993	30.6	3.2	25.9	1.4	0.1
Of which: United Kingdom	1988	16.3	2.9	10.7	0.9	1.8
	1989	17.1	4.2	11.1	1.1	0.6
	1990	8.6	5.6	2.0	0.9	0.1
	1991	19.4	4.7	14.7	—	0.1
	1992	18.2	1.9	17.1	−0.5	−0.3
	1993	18.2	1.7	16.8	−0.1	−0.1
Newly industrializing economies[1]	1988	2.8	2.1	−0.2	0.3	0.6
	1989	4.4	3.4	0.3	—	0.7
	1990	5.1	2.6	—	2.4	0.1
	1991	2.7	1.0	0.6	1.4	−0.3
	1992	−1.2	0.6	0.2	−0.9	−1.1
	1993	−1.3	0.3	0.1	−0.1	−1.6
Other	1988	30.1	7.4	8.3	10.3	4.1
	1989	45.1	9.7	18.6	12.8	4.0
	1990	41.2	8.8	16.3	11.4	4.7
	1991	34.2	6.5	17.2	9.0	1.5
	1992	10.0	4.3	−1.8	7.1	0.4
	1993	10.4	3.5	3.8	1.1	2.0
			In percent of total flow in 1988–93			
Total	—	100.0	100.0	100.0	100.0	100.0
United States	—	31.7	51.4	23.2	27.4	33.8
European Union	—	42.7	21.8	61.0	10.9	27.3
Of which: United Kingdom	—	13.7	11.2	18.1	2.5	5.6
Newly industrializing economies[1]	—	1.8	5.3	0.3	3.6	−4.4
Other	—	23.9	21.4	15.6	58.1	43.3

Source: Bank of Japan, *Balance of Payments Monthly* (Tokyo, various April issues).
[1]Hong Kong, Korea, Singapore, and Taiwan Province of China.

Table 3-4. Long-Term Capital Inflow by Region and Type

	Year	Total	Direct Investment	Securities	Loans	Other
			In billions of U.S. dollars			
Total	1988	19.0	−0.5	20.3	−0.1	−0.8
	1989	102.9	−1.1	85.1	17.8	1.0
	1990	77.2	1.8	34.7	39.1	1.7
	1991	158.5	1.4	115.3	38.1	3.7
	1992	29.5	2.7	8.2	15.9	2.7
	1993	−4.7	0.1	−11.1	4.3	1.9
United States	1988	2.2	−0.6	2.9	—	−0.1
	1989	3.3	−1.5	4.6	0.2	—
	1990	4.7	0.6	3.7	0.5	—
	1991	16.7	−0.1	16.6	0.2	−0.1
	1992	−4.4	0.8	−5.8	0.6	—
	1993	−25.0	0.5	−25.5	—	—
European Union	1988	21.4	0.1	21.4	—	—
	1989	98.7	0.3	92.2	6.2	—
	1990	35.7	1.1	30.1	4.6	—
	1991	88.7	0.6	86.2	1.8	—
	1992	19.6	1.3	17.3	0.9	—
	1993	12.5	−1.1	13.0	0.6	—
Of which: United Kingdom	1988	22.6	—	22.7	—	—
	1989	97.4	0.1	91.0	6.2	—
	1990	34.8	0.1	30.2	4.4	—
	1991	80.6	0.2	78.6	1.8	—
	1992	16.4	1.0	14.7	0.7	—
	1993	15.6	0.1	15.3	0.3	—
Newly industrializing economies[1]	1988	−5.2	—	−5.2	—	—
	1989	6.9	0.1	−4.6	11.5	—
	1990	32.9	0.1	−1.3	34.0	—
	1991	47.4	—	11.3	36.1	—
	1992	12.4	0.1	−2.1	14.3	—
	1993	2.4	0.2	−1.7	3.8	—
Other	1988	0.5	—	1.2	−0.1	−0.7
	1989	−6.1	0.1	−7.0	—	0.9
	1990	3.8	—	2.2	—	1.7
	1991	5.7	0.8	1.1	—	3.7
	1992	1.9	0.5	−1.2	—	2.7
	1993	5.4	0.4	3.1	—	1.9
			In percent of total flow in 1988–93			
Total	—	100.0	100.0	100.0	100.0	100.0
United States	—	−0.6	−6.7	−1.4	1.3	−1.1
European Union	—	72.4	54.3	103.1	12.2	—
Of which: United Kingdom	—	69.9	34.4	100.0	11.7	—
Newly industrializing economies[1]	—	25.3	12.2	−1.4	86.6	—
Other	—	3.0	40.2	−0.3	—	101.1

Source: Bank of Japan, *Balance of Payments Monthly* (Tokyo, various April issues).
[1]Hong Kong, Korea, Singapore, and Taiwan Province of China.

been insignificant, loans have been the only other important source of long-term capital inflow, particularly since 1989. European countries have been the source of the bulk of inward securities investment, and the newly industrializing economies have accounted for the largest share in loans to Japan.

With few exceptions, the regional pattern of net long-term capital flows is different from the pattern of trade flows, which is to be expected under a multilateral payments system and free capital movement (Table 3-5). In the case of the United States, the recent large bilateral trade surpluses in favor of Japan have been by and large matched by net exports of long-term capital from Japan to the United States. However, the United Kingdom, having had approximately balanced trade with Japan in 1988–93, and the newly industrializing economies, having run large trade deficits with Japan, were major sources of net inflow of long-term capital to Japan.[6] By contrast, the developing countries had a trade surplus with Japan and also were important recipients of Japanese long-term capital outflows.

Short-Term Capital Flows

The fluctuations in short-term capital flows have been even sharper than those in long-term flows (see Table 3-1). The net inflow, which had been negligible in the first half of the 1980s, surged in the second half to an average of $51 billion, peaking in 1987 at $96 billion. This increase mainly reflected the activities of private banks, which accumulated net foreign liabilities of $194 billion in 1985–89. Following a small net inflow in 1990, the short-term capital account turned to a large outflow position of $119 billion in 1991 and has remained in deficit since. Banks already had become net exporters of short-term capital in 1990, and by end-1993 they had reversed all of the massive run-up in net foreign liabilities during the second half of the 1980s. By contrast, almost half of the $85 billion increase in the nonbank private sector's net short-term liabilities in 1987–90 remains outstanding.

Flow of Financial Resources to Developing Countries

Although the bulk of Japan's large current account surpluses has been intermediated to other industrial countries through private sector financial institutions, especially institutional investors, a significant portion of the surpluses has also been transferred to developing countries, both by the Government and the private sector. Indeed, by 1987 net financial flows from Japan to developing

countries were the largest in the world, and since 1989 Japan has ranked first in official development assistance.

Since the mid-1980s, Japan has taken several initiatives to stimulate the flow of financial resources to the developing countries. The most comprehensive initiatives have been two multiyear plans—a capital recycling plan for 1987–92 amounting to $65 billion, and a "Funds for Development" initiative for 1993–97 with a target of $120 billion. The recycling plan pulled together official development assistance, other official flows, and private flows into one package, with official flows intended to serve as a catalyst for increased private flows, particularly to heavily indebted countries. Financing under that plan included direct bilateral lending, cofinancing with multilateral lending agencies, parallel lending with the IMF, and funds allocated to highly indebted countries under the strengthened debt strategy. The new $120 billion plan consists of $70 billion in untied official funds and $50 billion in other financing, including loans from the Export-Import Bank of Japan and international trade insurance.

In recent years, Japan's total net financial flows to developing countries have averaged $20 billion annually (Table 3-6). About half of the total has been accounted for by official development assistance, which takes the form of contributions to the multilateral financial institutions and bilateral loans, grants, and technical assistance. Other official flows, including loans by the Export-Import Bank of Japan, have been about 10 percent of the total. The remaining part has originated from the private sector, including loans from commercial banks, direct investment, and commercial bank cofinancing with the Export-Import Bank and with multilateral development institutions.

Japan's net disbursements of official development assistance amounted to about $11 billion a year in 1991–93. Although Japan remains the world's largest supplier of nonmilitary aid, its ratio of official assistance to GNP (0.26 percent in 1993) is slightly below the OECD's Development Assistance Committee average and falls well short of the United Nations target of 0.7 percent. The target for 1993–97 has been set at $70–75 billion, enhancing Japan's position as the largest donor over the medium term but implying little change in the aid-to-GNP ratio. The new plan is the first implemented by the Government since an Official Development Assistance Charter was adopted in 1992. The Charter outlines four principles that mandate more stringent conditions for foreign aid. They stipulate that Japan must pay close attention to the following issues: environmental concerns; restraint in military expenditures and weapons development; democratization and human rights; and the fostering of market-oriented economies.

The regional allocation of Japan's official assistance is well diversified. Although Asia receives the bulk of Japan's bilateral aid—with Indonesia, China, the Philippines, India, and Thailand accounting for over 40 percent

---

[6] The regional pattern of capital flows is distorted by the existence of offshore markets, especially those in London, Luxembourg, Hong Kong, and Singapore.

Table 3-5. Net Long-Term Capital Outflow by Region and Type
(In billions of U.S. dollars)

	Year	Total	Direct Investment	Securities	Loans	Other
Total	1988	130.9	34.7	66.7	15.3	14.3
	1989	89.2	45.2	28.0	4.7	11.3
	1990	43.6	46.3	5.0	−16.9	9.2
	1991	−37.1	29.4	−41.0	−25.0	−0.4
	1992	28.5	14.5	26.2	−8.3	−4.0
	1993	78.3	13.6	62.7	3.8	−1.9
United States	1988	59.3	19.6	33.3	2.8	3.5
	1989	53.9	22.8	22.1	4.8	4.3
	1990	11.7	25.0	−19.8	2.8	3.8
	1991	18.4	15.3	−1.0	2.6	1.5
	1992	27.2	8.1	14.3	4.2	0.6
	1993	58.9	6.2	47.4	5.7	−0.5
European Union	1988	34.1	5.7	21.2	1.8	5.4
	1989	−13.2	9.4	−24.6	−1.4	3.3
	1990	22.2	9.9	9.4	0.6	2.3
	1991	−39.2	7.3	−45.3	−1.8	0.6
	1992	6.7	2.0	10.1	−4.3	−1.2
	1993	18.1	4.3	12.8	0.9	0.1
Of which: United Kingdom	1988	−6.3	2.9	−12.0	0.9	1.8
	1989	−80.3	4.1	−79.8	−5.1	0.6
	1990	−26.1	5.5	−28.2	−3.5	0.1
	1991	−61.2	4.4	−63.9	−1.8	0.1
	1992	1.8	0.9	2.3	−1.2	−0.3
	1993	2.6	1.6	1.5	−0.4	−0.1
Newly industrializing economies[1]	1988	8.0	2.1	5.0	0.3	0.6
	1989	−2.5	3.3	4.9	−11.5	0.7
	1990	−27.7	2.6	1.3	−31.7	0.1
	1991	−44.7	1.0	−10.7	−34.7	−0.3
	1992	−13.5	0.5	2.4	−15.2	−1.1
	1993	−3.7	0.1	1.8	−3.9	−1.6

of the total—Africa, the Middle East, and Latin America are also major recipient areas (Egypt, Jordan, Turkey, and Peru have recently been among the top ten recipients of aid). Japan is now the leading donor in some 30 developing countries, not only in Asia but also in parts of Africa.

Foreign Direct Investment

Japanese outward FDI surged in the second half of the 1980s, with the stock of overseas investment growing almost fivefold between 1985 and 1992 (Chart 3-3). This spectacular increase prompts a number of questions:

- Was the increase in FDI particular to Japan, or was it part of a worldwide spurt in FDI? Is Japan's FDI unusually large by international standards?
- What is the regional and sectoral distribution of Japanese FDI, and how has the pattern changed over the

years? To what extent was the rapid growth in the second half of the 1980s attributable to investment in real estate and financial institutions in the United States?

- What have been the main factors responsible for the rapid growth in FDI? Is the increase a natural part of the process of industrial restructuring, or did it occur in response to government intervention (tax policy, trade barriers) or because of macroeconomic factors (yen appreciation, asset price bubble)?
- What are the salient characteristics of Japanese overseas subsidiaries? Do Japanese affiliates differ from those involved in other countries' FDI, with respect to profitability, repatriation rates, imports, and destination of production?
- What have been the main effects of Japanese FDI on other economies? Has Japanese investment created jobs and promoted growth in the host countries, and has it been a drain on these countries' trade accounts?

Table 3-5 (concluded)

	Year	Total	Direct Investment	Securities	Loans	Other
Other	1988	29.6	7.4	7.1	10.3	4.8
	1989	51.1	9.7	25.6	12.8	3.1
	1990	37.4	8.8	14.2	11.4	3.0
	1991	28.5	5.7	16.1	9.0	−2.2
	1992	8.1	3.9	−0.6	7.1	−2.2
	1993	5.0	3.1	0.7	1.1	0.2
			Average, 1988–93[2]			
Total						
Current account	—	82.4	—	—	—	—
Long-term capital account	—	55.6	—	—	—	—
United States						
Current account	—	45.3	—	—	—	—
Long-term capital account	—	38.2	—	—	—	—
European Union						
Current account	—	21.3	—	—	—	—
Long-term capital account	—	4.8	—	—	—	—
Of which: United Kingdom						
Current account	—	0.5	—	—	—	—
Long-term capital account	—	−28.3	—	—	—	—
Newly industrializing economies[1]						
Current account	—	30.8	—	—	—	—
Long-term capital account	—	−14.0	—	—	—	—
Other						
Current account	—	−15.0	—	—	—	—
Long-term capital account	—	26.6	—	—	—	—

Source: Bank of Japan, *Balance of Payments Monthly* (Tokyo, various April issues).
[1]Hong Kong, Korea, Singapore, and Taiwan Province of China.
[2]Current account surplus in favor of Japan, and net long-term capital outflow from Japan.

- Has FDI had a significant impact on Japan's economy, especially the external surplus? Are Japanese exports and FDI complementary, or does FDI generate increased imports from overseas subsidiaries? Does income from direct investment provide a significant contribution to foreign exchange receipts?

These issues will be addressed in the remainder of this section, preceded by a discussion of the concept and measurement of FDI and a review of main developments since the 1950s.

Concept and Measurement

Conceptually, FDI refers to an investment made by a foreign resident to acquire a controlling interest in a host-country company (IMF (1992, p. 24)). It is the motive of the investment—corporate control—that distinguishes FDI from portfolio investment, which is simply the estab-

lishment of a claim on an asset for the purpose of realizing a return without being involved in management.

In practice, capital inflows designated as direct investment are distinguished from portfolio investment solely on the basis of percentage of foreign ownership. At present, the international standard (also followed by Japan) is a cross-border holding of 10 percent or more of the voting power in an incorporated enterprise (or a similar interest in an unincorporated enterprise). Although the 10 percent ownership criterion is arbitrary, it is unlikely to be an important source of measurement errors (Graham and Krugman (1991, pp. 7–11) and IMF (1992, pp. 24–25)). For example, foreign companies with operations in the United States own on average an 80 percent share of their affiliates, suggesting that for most of these affiliates foreign ownership is both clear in practice and accurately recorded in balance of payments statistics (Froot (1991)). FDI data, however, tend to understate actual foreign control because they do not include investment by foreign

Table 3-6. Net Flow of Financial Resources to Developing Countries and Multilateral Agencies from Japan[1]

	1987	1988	1989	1990	1991	1992	Est. 1993
	In billions of U.S. dollars						
Official development assistance	7.5	9.1	9.0	9.1	11.0	11.2	11.3
Bilateral	5.2	6.4	6.8	6.8	8.9	8.4	...
Loans	3.0	3.5	3.7	3.8	5.5	4.6	...
Grants and other	2.2	2.9	3.1	3.0	3.3	3.8	...
Multilateral	2.2	2.7	2.2	2.3	2.1	2.8	...
Other official flows	−1.8	−0.6	1.6	3.4	2.6	3.3	...
Export credit	−2.0	−1.8	−1.2	−1.0	−0.5	0.1	...
Direct investment	0.3	1.4	1.9	4.2	3.2	2.1	...
Multilateral	—	−0.2	0.9	0.3	0.1	1.1	...
Private flows	14.7	12.8	14.3	6.3	11.2	1.5	...
Export credit	1.1	0.2	0.7	—	0.6	−1.0	...
Direct investment	7.4	8.2	11.3	8.1	5.0	2.8	...
Other bilateral	4.4	2.8	1.3	−2.6	6.2	2.8	...
Multilateral	1.9	1.6	0.2	0.7	−0.7	−3.0	...
Grants by private voluntary agencies	0.1	0.1	0.1	0.1	0.2	0.2	...
Total resource flows	20.5	21.4	25.6	18.7	24.9	16.2	...
	In percent of GNP						
Official development assistance	0.31	0.32	0.31	0.31	0.32	0.30	0.26
Total resource flows	0.86	0.75	0.84	0.63	0.73	0.44	...

Source: Japanese authorities.
[1]Calendar years; Development Assistance Committee (OECD) basis.

affiliates that is financed by selling securities to unrelated parties (domestic or foreign). Furthermore, official statistics record only the book value of the FDI and do not allow for increases in the value of foreign-controlled assets.

There are two main sources of data on Japanese FDI. The Bank of Japan compiles monthly balance of payments data, with no breakdown by industry but with some aggregated breakdown by host country made available on an annual basis. The Ministry of Finance publishes annual flow and stock data on FDI on a notification basis, with a detailed breakdown by industry and host country. These data tend to overstate the actual amount of FDI because some investment announced is not actually undertaken and because implementation may follow notification with a considerable lag. In recent years, the annual inflows of FDI as reported by the Ministry of Finance have been about 50 percent larger than those recorded in the balance of payments by the Bank of Japan (see Chart 3-3). In addition to these two main data sources, the Ministry of International Trade and Industry (MITI) conducts questionnaire surveys on Japanese enterprises' activities abroad. These surveys provide information on the market destination of Japanese FDI and on cross-border intrafirm trade. The following discussion mainly uses balance of payments data, so that international comparisons can be made. Ministry of Finance data are used in analyzing the regional and sectoral composition of FDI and are supplemented by results from MITI surveys.

Main Developments

Japanese postwar FDI was conducted only on a small scale until the early 1970s, in part because of stringent government regulations imposed because of the weak balance of payments. According to balance of payments data, annual outflows rose slowly, to an average of $150 million in the second half of the 1960s, and at end-1970

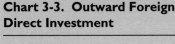

Chart 3-3. Outward Foreign Direct Investment

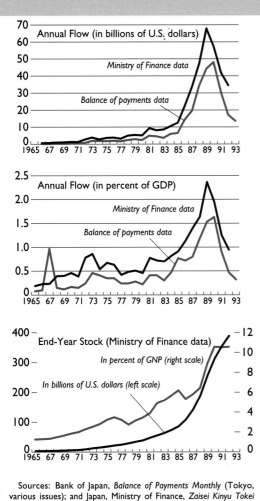

Sources: Bank of Japan, *Balance of Payments Monthly* (Tokyo, various issues); and Japan, Ministry of Finance, *Zaisei Kinyu Tokei Geppo* (Tokyo, various issues).

plus. This led not only to the easing of government regulations on FDI but also to a policy to promote it: restrictions on FDI were eased in four steps in 1969–72; the Export-Import Bank of Japan lowered interest rates on loans for foreign investment; and, in order to reduce the risks of FDI, tax provisions for overseas investment loss reserves were revised (Komiya and Wakasugi (1991, p. 51)). As regards the pattern of Japanese FDI in the 1970s, the share of mining declined substantially, and large investments were made in the U.S. distribution sector to support the marketing of exports of automobiles and other durable goods. Nevertheless, developing countries continued to host the bulk of Japanese FDI.

During the 1980s, Japan's FDI grew spectacularly. In the first half of the decade, overseas investment increased briskly, tripling to $6.5 billion (½ of 1 percent of GDP) between 1980 and 1985. Even more extraordinary growth was experienced in the second half of the decade. Japanese FDI during the four-year period 1986–89 exceeded the cumulative overseas investment from all postwar years combined. By the late 1980s, Japan's FDI outflow had become the largest in the world, and a peak outflow of $48 billion (1½ percent of GDP) was reached in 1990. At that time, the annual flow was 20 times larger than a decade before, and the stock of FDI stood at $302 billion (10 percent of GDP) compared with $48 billion (4 percent of GDP) in 1980.

The unprecedented growth in FDI in the late 1980s was accompanied by a substantial change in the pattern of overseas investment. During the 1980s, the share of Japanese FDI in manufacturing declined sharply, whereas the tertiary sectors, which had earlier accounted for less than half of the total, gained a combined share of more than 70 percent. Overseas investment increased particularly fast in finance and insurance, transport, and real estate, all of which had played only a minor role in Japanese FDI before the 1980s. Regionally, the share of developing countries (not only in Africa and Latin America but also in Asia) declined sharply, whereas industrial countries absorbed over two thirds of Japanese FDI, with the United States alone receiving over 40 percent of the investment.

The boom in Japanese FDI came to an end in the early 1990s, with the annual outflow declining steadily from the peak of $48 billion (1½ percent of GDP) in 1990 to $14 billion (⅓ of 1 percent of GDP) in 1993. Although the outflows were still large in absolute terms, relative to GDP they marked a return to the level first reached in the early 1970s. The regional and sectoral pattern of FDI remained broadly the same as in the years of rapid growth. The latest surveys of FDI intentions suggest that future areas of growth in Japanese overseas investment will be machinery, chemicals, and automobiles, with Asian countries (especially China and the members of the Association of South-East Asian Nations, ASEAN) likely to receive an increasing share of total Japanese FDI.

the stock of FDI was about 2 percent of that year's GDP. During this period, Japanese FDI took two principal forms. One was the acquisition of raw materials (especially mining products) to supply manufacturing industries in resources-short Japan. The other was foreign investment in labor-intensive manufacturing activities in the nearby Asian countries. Overall, almost two thirds of Japanese FDI in the 1950s and 1960s went to developing countries (Table 3-7).

In the early 1970s, Japanese FDI surged, rising fivefold between 1971 and 1973 before stabilizing at around $2 billion for the remainder of the decade. The large increase was induced in part by an improvement in Japan's current account position, which turned into a sur-

Table 3-7. Foreign Direct Investment by Region and Industry
(In percent of total)

			By Region						
Period	United States	All	Asia (newly industrializing economies)	Europe	Latin America	Middle East	Oceania	Other	Total
1951–60	30.7	17.3	4.6	1.1	30.0	19.8	0.7	0.4	100.0
1961–70	18.6	21.3	5.0	19.3	15.3	8.4	7.6	8.5	100.0
1971–75	22.0	28.1	10.2	15.2	17.5	5.2	5.3	6.1	100.0
1976–80	26.6	27.3	10.2	9.5	16.6	6.2	7.8	6.0	100.0
1981–85	34.8	20.4	8.7	13.9	20.1	1.5	3.6	5.7	100.0
1986–90	46.3	12.4	6.9	21.2	10.9	0.2	6.1	2.9	100.0
1991–92	42.1	16.3	5.4	21.7	8.0	1.1	7.5	3.3	100.0
1951–92	42.0	15.5	7.1	19.6	12.0	1.1	6.2	3.6	100.0

			By Industry						
	Manufacturing	Agriculture, forestry, and fishery	Mining	Commerce	Finance and insurance	Transport	Real estate	Other	Total
1951–60	44.9	2.5	30.4	11.3	3.9	—	—	7.1	100.0
1961–70	24.7	2.7	31.8	10.7	9.4	—	—	20.9	100.0
1971–75	33.3	2.0	25.1	14.8	8.0	—	0.1	16.7	100.0
1976–80	36.7	2.7	15.4	15.6	5.5	—	1.7	22.4	100.0
1981–85	25.1	0.7	9.9	15.4	17.9	12.5	5.4	13.1	100.0
1986–90	25.5	0.4	2.1	8.3	24.3	5.2	19.3	14.9	100.0
1990–92	29.9	0.8	3.0	12.0	12.8	5.6	18.8	17.1	100.0
1951–92	27.4	0.7	5.0	10.6	19.7	5.7	15.8	15.1	100.0

Source: Japan, Ministry of Finance, *Taigai chyokusetsu-toshi no kyoka todokede zisseki* (Tokyo, various issues).

Worldwide Perspective

The recent surge in FDI was not simply a Japanese phenomenon (Chart 3-4). World FDI rose sharply in the second half of the 1980s, both in absolute terms (to a peak of $238 billion in 1990) and relative to output (from a long-term average of ½ of 1 percent of GDP to over 1 percent of GDP in 1989–90). As in Japan, world FDI has been on a declining trend so far in the 1990s. The rapid growth of world FDI in the second half of the 1980s can be attributed in part to easing of restrictions on capital movements, deregulation of financial markets, and a lagged adjustment to exchange rate misalignments.

The growth in Japan's overseas investment in the 1980s was, however, faster than that in the other major industrial countries (Chart 3-5). In absolute terms, Japan had been the fourth largest direct investor in the 1970s (behind the United States, the United Kingdom, and Germany), accounting on average for 5 percent of world FDI. In the early 1980s, Japan moved to the top three, and during 1989–91 it was the world's leading direct investor, with a share of as much as 20 percent of the total. Even during these peak years, Japan's overseas investment relative to the size of the economy was low in comparison with other major industrial countries (except the United States). Moreover, despite large recent FDI outflows, Japanese overseas subsidiaries produce a relatively small share of the parent companies' output in comparison with affiliates of other industrial countries. In 1989, overseas production accounted for only 5 percent of the total sales of Japanese manufacturing corporations, compared with 15–20 percent for the United States and a number of European countries.

Although Japanese overseas investment flows have long been at levels comparable with other industrial countries, Japan remains an outlier in terms of inward FDI, with an insignificant share of the world total FDI going to Japan (Chart 3-6). Nevertheless, in contrast to developments in outward investment, Japanese inward FDI has risen steadily in recent years, from an annual average of $200 million in the 1980s to an average $1½ billion in 1990–93.

Chart 3-4. Japanese and World Direct Investment Outflows

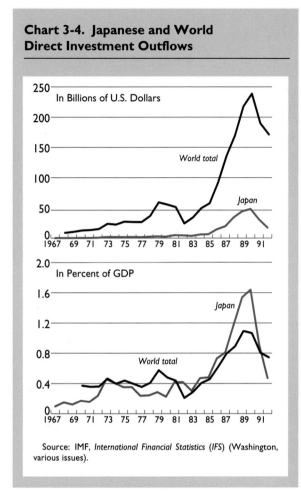

Source: IMF, *International Financial Statistics (IFS)* (Washington, various issues).

Chart 3-5. Direct Investment Outflows Among Five Major Industrial Countries

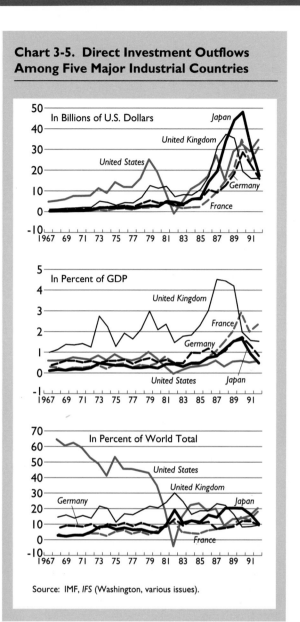

Source: IMF, *IFS* (Washington, various issues).

Determinants of Japanese Outward Foreign Direct Investment

There are two main approaches to explaining FDI: micro (industrial organization) theories, and macro (cost-of-capital) theories.[7] The industrial-organization view emphasizes that firm-specific intangible assets—such as patents, brand names, superior technology, and organizational skills—may under certain circumstances make it profitable for a firm to internalize the rents on these advantages through overseas investment, rather than through licensing or exports. According to this view, the presence of transaction costs in markets for intermediate goods, the desire to keep technological secrets, and attempts to circumvent trade restrictions are examples of

possible reasons for direct investment. The cost-of-capital view, by contrast, holds that if an investment is made by a foreign firm, rather than a domestic company, it may be because the foreign firm has a lower cost of capital and therefore requires lower returns.[8] In that case, incentives for FDI can be provided by the liberalization of capital markets, exchange rate movements, and

---

[7] For surveys of alternative theories of FDI, see Agarwal (1980), Kojima and Ozawa (1984), Jones and Neary (1986), Graham and Krugman (1991, pp. 35-38 and Appendix B), and Lizondo (1991). Empirical studies are surveyed in Mann (1993) and United Nations (1992).

[8] This characterization of the macroeconomic view is that of Graham and Krugman (1991, p. 35). These authors also describe the microeconomic view as suggesting that when foreign rather than domestic firms make the investment it is because they expect higher returns—that is, the investment is expected to be more profitable in foreign hands.

Chart 3-6. Direct Investment Inflows Among Five Major Industrial Countries

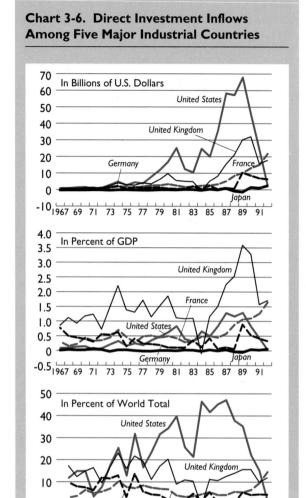

Source: IMF, *IFS* (Washington, various issues).

the industrial-organization and cost-of-capital explanations has important implications (Graham and Krugman (1991, p. 38)). If overseas investment is motivated purely by industrial-organization considerations, Japan's FDI has little to do with the transfer of Japan's surplus saving. However, if macroeconomic factors are behind Japan's overseas investment, future FDI flows are to some extent linked to prospects for the current account. Most studies agree that both approaches are relevant to explaining the rapid growth of Japan's overseas investment in the 1980s and its subsequent decline.[9]

Proponents of the microeconomic approach point out that much of Japanese FDI has been in response to industrial restructuring and evolving comparative advantage. As mentioned above, in the 1950s and 1960s, the bulk of Japanese overseas investment was in the areas of natural resource acquisition and labor-intensive manufacturing. The FDI in natural resource extraction represented a form of backward vertical integration by Japanese users of raw materials or by Japanese trading companies having close links to them. Similarly, the investment in manufacturing in nearby Asian countries represented a transfer of production abroad in a sector where Japan was losing comparative advantage. In the 1970s, the heavy investments in the distribution sector to support the marketing of consumer durables, especially automobiles, were a form of forward vertical integration by Japanese manufacturers. As noted by Caves (1993), these investments were in accordance with the standard theory of FDI based on transaction costs, with controlled-distribution subsidiaries displacing arm's-length distributors. As regards the more recent period, empirical studies (such as Kogut and Chang (1991) and Hennart and Park (1991)) have established a positive relationship between the rapid growth of research and development expenditure by Japanese firms and Japan's FDI, consistent with the industrial-organization view that overseas investment takes place to arbitrage intangible assets (specific advantages) accumulated by firms in the source country.[10]

The industrial-organization literature on FDI also regards circumventing trade restrictions (existing or prospective) as an important explanation for Japanese FDI. Increased protection reduces a foreign company's net revenues from exporting, raising the relative profitability of foreign investment and turning the exporter into a

macroeconomic policies (especially monetary and tax measures), among other things.

Lower costs of production in the host country compared with the source country—a factor often mentioned in popular discussions—*alone* cannot be a reason for FDI. If, say, labor is relatively cheap in the host country, it is cheap for domestic and foreign firms alike. Hence, foreign firms, rather than domestic ones, will carry out the investment more profitably only if they possess specific advantages, such as those mentioned above under the micro and macro approaches.

How well do the micro and macro approaches explain developments in Japan's FDI? The distinction between

---

[9] See, for example, Barrell and Pain (1993), Caves (1993), Froot (1991), Georgiou and Weinhold (1992), Graham and Krugman (1991), Mann (1993), and Thomsen (1993).

[10] Kogut and Chang (1991) also found Japanese FDI to the United States to increase with the intensity of research and development of the industries in the United States. The positive effect of U.S. research and development on Japanese FDI could indicate that Japanese firms come to acquire intangible assets and not just to exploit those already in their possession.

direct investor.[11] As surveyed by Caves (1993, p. 290), there is a wealth of evidence from econometric and case studies that trade restrictions in the United States have had a significant positive effect on FDI from Japan. In particular, voluntary export restraints in the automobile sector and the 1986 semiconductor trade agreement have been shown to induce sizable direct investment flows from Japan. As for Japanese FDI to the EU, the evidence is less clear-cut (see Thomsen (1993, pp. 306–09)). Many studies, including Barrell and Pain (1993) and Heitger and Stehn (1990), have found protection in the EU or the prospect of a single European market (or both) to have been an important determinant of Japanese FDI to the EU; however, some (notably Nicolaides and Thomsen (1991)) have suggested that preparation for the single market affected mainly the timing, rather than the long-run level, of direct investment in the EU. Besides the United States and the EU, trade restrictions also motivated some of Japan's FDI in other Asian countries, the exports of which were not subject to the trade barriers aimed at Japanese exporters.

Although industrial-organization considerations may well explain a major part of Japan's trend FDI and some of the increase in Japanese FDI in the 1980s, most analysts agree that macroeconomic factors are also needed to explain the increase.[12] Indeed, the purchase of property abroad (which was responsible for 24 percent of the increase in Japanese FDI in 1986–90) and part of the investment in banking and finance, though recorded as direct investment, are clearly more akin to portfolio investment and therefore unrelated to industrial-organization motives.[13] Among the macroeconomic determinants, three factors seem to have played key roles: the appreciation of the yen; the extraordinary rise in asset prices; and liberalization of foreign exchange controls. Albeit potentially important, changes in tax policy and the business cycle do not appear to have had a significant effect.

Between the fall of 1985 and late 1988, the yen appreciated by 42 percent in real effective terms. This strengthening of the yen brought about a sharp decline in the cost of production and investment in host countries relative to the cost in Japan, raising the profitability of direct investment. Exchange rate appreciation also worked through other channels to increase FDI. For example, with a stronger yen, Japanese firms, whose book values

rose compared with those of foreign companies, were able to collateralize assets to finance new investment more easily than were their competitors in countries with depreciated currencies (Froot and Stein (1991)). This enabled Japanese investors to pay higher prices than liquidity-constrained bidders in host countries. Another possible channel, often mentioned in popular discussions but implying irrational behavior, is that Japanese investors may have focused on the comparatively low prices of physical assets in host countries with depreciated currencies, neglecting the question of whether the economic returns were equivalent (Graham and Krugman (1991, p. 46)). Whatever the transmission mechanism, empirical studies, such as those by Caves (1989), Froot and Stein (1991), and Mann (1993), have typically found a significant positive relationship between exchange rate appreciation and outward FDI.

In the second half of the 1980s, the Japanese economy experienced an asset price bubble during which land prices doubled and stock prices tripled.[14] The spectacular price increases were in part driven by an easy monetary policy, and they enabled Japanese companies to increase their overseas investment both through lower cost of capital and through additional liquidity. The increased liquidity was created by Japanese banks, which could count 45 percent of their large, unrealized capital gains on stockholdings as capital, enabling them to lend more than competitors elsewhere. The borrowers, including companies engaged in FDI, could in turn use high-priced land and equities as collateral to increase their investment. As noted by Graham and Krugman (1991, p. 47), to the extent that the asset price increases represented a bubble, the lower cost of capital can be interpreted as a subsidy to Japanese firms investing abroad that was paid by those who bought the overpriced stocks and land.

Liberalization of capital controls, described in the first part of this section, also contributed to the spurt of FDI in the 1980s. Although Japanese enterprises in manufacturing, commerce, and services were generally free to undertake FDI even before the revision of foreign exchange laws in December 1980, after the revision financial and insurance firms also became free to invest abroad. In the event, FDI in finance and insurance came to account for 31 percent of the increase in Japanese FDI in 1986–90.

Changes in corporate taxation, particularly in the United States and Japan, provide another possible (but probably not a major) explanation for developments in Japan's FDI since 1980. According to the Japanese tax system, foreign subsidiaries of Japanese firms pay corporate taxes in the host country. However, when they repatriate income to their parent company, they are liable to

---

[11] The "tariff-jumping" or "defensive" FDI hypothesis that firms invest abroad to avoid trade barriers was introduced by Mundell (1957). He used a traditional Heckscher-Ohlin trade model to show that when one country imposes a tariff on its importable (capital-intensive) good, this will generate an inflow of capital from the other country that will substitute for trade.

[12] See Barrell and Pain (1993), Caves (1993), Froot (1991), Georgiou and Weinhold (1992), Graham and Krugman (1991), Komiya and Wakasugi (1991), and Thomsen (1993).

[13] See Tabata (1990) for a discussion of Japanese banks' FDI to the United States.

---

[14] See Section VI of this volume for a description and analysis of the asset price bubble.

taxation at the Japanese rate, with a credit for taxes paid abroad. Under this system, a cut in the corporate tax rate abroad puts host-country firms, which receive the full benefit of the tax cut, at an advantage relative to the subsidiaries of Japanese firms, whose lower foreign tax liability would be offset by an increased liability in Japan. Thus, the 1981 corporate tax cuts in the United States, notably the introduction of accelerated depreciation, acted as a disincentive to Japanese FDI in the United States, whereas the 1986 tax reform, which eliminated the special investment incentives, removed this bias against foreign ownership (Graham and Krugman (1991, pp. 47–49)). Similarly, changes in the corporate tax rate in Japan affect the incentives of Japanese firms to invest overseas. The most significant change in Japan's corporate taxation in recent years was a 4.5 percentage point cut in the corporate tax rate in 1990, which improved the profitability of domestic investment and therefore should have discouraged outward FDI. Although the above-mentioned tax changes in the United States and Japan are likely to have made some contribution to the ups and downs of Japanese FDI over the past decade, empirical studies (reviewed in Iwamoto (1990)) typically find taxation to have played only a subsidiary role.

The business cycle has also been mentioned as a determinant of FDI (Graham and Krugman (1991, pp. 50–1)). There is no obvious reason for cyclical fluctuations to affect the share of foreign control in the host country in a systematic way. However, the balance of payments measure of FDI includes intrafirm financing, which is affected by economic prospects and financing conditions in both the source and host countries. Indeed, simple regressions suggest that world FDI behaves procyclically, rising faster than world output during periods of recovery and falling faster during recessions. Thus, the economic boom in Japan and other major industrial countries in the second half of the 1980s could have been responsible for some of the rapid increase in Japanese FDI. Given that the growth of FDI was many times faster than that of output, other factors are likely to have played a more important role.

What explains the marked decline in Japanese overseas investment after 1990? It is difficult to pinpoint industrial-organization factors that might have played a role, but the reversal of a number of macroeconomic developments seems to provide a plausible explanation: the real effective value of the yen depreciated by 22 percent between late 1988 and mid-1990 and, despite subsequent gradual appreciation, remained below the earlier peak until 1993; the asset price bubble collapsed, with land and equity prices returning to trend levels by 1993; the stock adjustment to the removal of capital controls was likely to have been completed by the early 1990s; and the Japanese economy has been in recession since mid-1991. It is still too early to tell whether the marked appreciation of the yen in 1993–94 will induce another burst of Japanese FDI in the mid-1990s.

Characteristics of Japanese Overseas Subsidiaries

As discussed above, standard industrial-organization and cost-of-capital theories seem to go a long way toward explaining the main developments in Japan's FDI. Some observers have noted, however, that the overseas affiliates of Japanese companies differ from those of other countries in several respects. They have a greater propensity to import—for example, Japanese manufacturing subsidiaries import three times as much per worker as do other foreign manufacturing affiliates in the United States, which themselves are more import-intensive than domestic companies (Graham and Krugman (1991, p. 78)). The Japanese parent companies import relatively less from their affiliates and strongly direct their interfirm exports to their foreign distribution subsidiaries. Japanese companies have also displayed a marked (but diminishing) preference to establish their investments by building a new facility ("greenfield" investment) instead of acquiring control of an existing company (Caves (1993, p. 291)). Furthermore, the affiliates' profitability is low compared with that of U.S. firms. The following average profit rates for 1983–88 were adapted from Komiya and Wakasugi (1991):[15] Japanese-owned overseas subsidiaries, 0.4 percent (average for all Japanese corporations, 0.9 percent); U.S.-owned overseas subsidiaries, 5.0 percent (average for all U.S. corporations, 2.7 percent).

The differences can probably be attributed primarily to the more recent origin of Japanese FDI rather than to any difference in the underlying microeconomic behavior. Because of the recent rapid growth of Japanese FDI, the average Japanese affiliate has been in operation for a far shorter time than its counterpart from other countries, let alone the average domestic competitor. There is little evidence to suggest that the above-mentioned differences will persist once Japanese FDI matures. Nevertheless, the possibility that reasons such as corporate group (keiretsu) relationships contribute to these differences cannot be excluded.

Effects of Japanese Foreign Direct Investment on Other Economies

The general effects of foreign direct investment are well known. In the absence of distortions, FDI generates net benefits. These benefits include not only the usual gains from trade and international integration—exploitation of comparative advantage, a larger and more efficient scale of production, and increased competition—but also positive externalities in the host economy in the form of new technology, work force skills, and management techniques (Graham and Krugman (1991), Nicolaides (1991), and Georgiou and Weinhold (1992)).

---

[15] Profits after taxes, divided by sales.

Despite the general presumption that FDI is beneficial, concern has been expressed that foreign investment carries costs for the host country. The adverse effects of FDI are often claimed to include loss of employment and negative trade balance effects. Critics of FDI argue that as foreign-owned companies tend to be import intensive, their activities will result in reduced demand for domestic products, which will cost jobs. In turn, advocates of FDI point to anecdotal evidence that foreign-owned companies employ a large number of workers and account for a significant share of job creation in many countries. For example, Japanese-owned manufacturing companies employ 100,000 Europeans (Thomsen (1993, p. 302)). In the United States, employment in Japanese-controlled firms increased by 428,000 workers between 1977 and 1989 (Graham and Krugman (1991, p. 26)), and in 1987–89 one third of all new manufacturing jobs were the result of Japanese FDI.

Both of these anecdotal views are somewhat misleading because they are based on partial equilibrium analyses. To be sure, foreign investment, like investment by domestic companies, will cause changes in the distribution of employment within the country and across industries, but the net effect on employment is likely to be small beyond the short run. To the extent that FDI has no influence on potential output and the natural rate of unemployment, it should not affect the long-run level of employment. If there is any long-run effect, however, it is likely to be positive: FDI may enhance potential output, and thereby employment, through the externalities discussed earlier.

That Japanese-owned firms tend to have a higher propensity to import than do their host-country counterparts has prompted critics to claim that Japanese FDI worsens the external position of host countries. This criticism is again based on partial equilibrium considerations: if production by Japanese affiliates crowds out domestic firms with a lower import content, the sectoral trade balance will worsen in the short run.[16] Standard macroeconomic theory suggests, however, that any permanent effects of FDI on the aggregate current account balance are likely to be small (Graham and Krugman (1991, pp. 63–4)). By definition, the current account position is the difference between domestic saving and domestic investment. Changes in import propensities, like other microeconomic factors, cannot influence the current account unless they affect the fundamental determinants of saving or investment. However, the higher import propensity of Japanese affiliates will, if sustained, put downward pressure on host-country currencies. A depreciated exchange rate will compensate for the higher im-

port intensity, encouraging exports, discouraging imports, and thereby leaving the overall current account position (but not sectoral trade balances) unchanged. Estimates for the United States, the main destination for Japan's FDI, suggest that the quantitative importance of the increased share of foreign control on the value of the dollar is small (Graham and Krugman (1991, pp. 69–70)).

Effects on Japan

The discussion in the previous subsection underscores that, in the long run, overseas investment should have little effect on Japan's employment and current account balance: adjustments in the domestic labor market will bring aggregate employment to the "natural" level, and exchange rate changes will keep the external position, as determined by saving and investment behavior, unchanged. Much attention in Japan has, however, been paid to the influence of growing outward FDI on the trade balance in the short term and medium run (see, for example, Dai-ichi Kangyo Bank (1994) and Japan Research Institute (1990)).

A stylized (partial equilibrium) view of the impact of FDI on the trade balance can be summarized as follows. In the early stages of overseas production, the trade balance is likely to improve, owing to exports of capital goods and intermediate inputs from Japan to the newly established subsidiaries abroad. Later, the trade balance starts to decline, both because of reverse imports (exports to Japan by subsidiaries abroad) and because goods produced by overseas subsidiaries replace exports in local or third-country markets. The latter negative effect on the trade balance is in part offset by decreased imports of inputs for the relaced exports. Similar to the J-curve effect of exchange rate changes, this sequence of movements in the trade surplus is sometimes called the "overseas investment J-curve effect."

In the long run, once (general equilibrium) adjustments in the exchange rate in response to FDI flows have taken place, the presumption is that the trade balance will be worse than in the absence of FDI by an amount equivalent to the repatriated profits of the subsidiaries. An indication of the magnitude of the likely long-run effect of FDI on Japan's trade account is obtained by looking at recent trends in overseas direct investment income (Chart 3-7). Between 1978 and 1993, direct investment income from Japanese-owned companies abroad increased tenfold, to over $8 billion. Income from direct investment has also risen relative to the size of the economy, but still amounts to only about 0.2 percent of GDP. The return on FDI (ratio of repatriated profits to the stock of FDI) has, however, declined to about 3 percent in recent years, compared with an average of 6 percent until the mid-1980s. Assuming that this decline, which is likely to reflect the usual lags between investment and profits, is reversed and that direct investment grows in line with

---

[16] Partial equilibrium arguments could also lead to the opposite conclusion: if an FDI project has been undertaken to replace exports with host-country production (perhaps to circumvent trade restrictions), the trade balance of the host country will improve.

Chart 3-7. Direct Investment Income

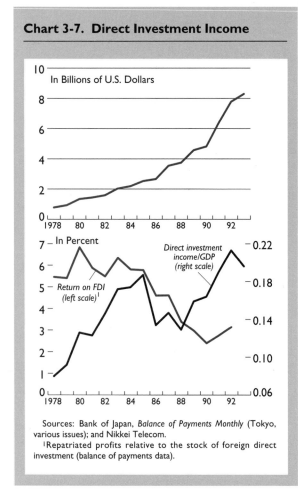

Sources: Bank of Japan, *Balance of Payments Monthly* (Tokyo, various issues); and Nikkei Telecom.
[1]Repatriated profits relative to the stock of foreign direct investment (balance of payments data).

GDP, investment income from FDI could rise to 0.4 percent of GDP.

References

Agarwal, Jamuna P., "Determinants of Foreign Direct Investment: A Survey," *Weltwirtschafliches Archiv*, Vol. 116, Heft 4 (1980).

Barrell, Ray and Nigel Pain, "Trade Restraints and Japanese Direct Investment Flows," National Institute of Economic and Social Research Discussion Paper 43 (London, March 1993).

Caves, Richard E., "Exchange Rate Movements and Foreign Direct Investment in the United States," in *The Internationalization of U.S. Markets*, edited by D.B. Audretsch and M.P. Claudon (New York: New York University Press, 1989), pp. 199–228.

———, "Japanese Investment in the United States: Lessons for the Economic Analysis of Foreign Investment," *World Economy*, Vol. 16 (May 1993), pp. 279–300.

Dai-ichi Kangyo Bank, "Japan's Overseas Direct Investments at a Turning Point," *DKB Economic Report*, Vol. 24 (February 15, 1994).

French, Kenneth R., and James M. Poterba, "Investor Diversification and International Equity Markets," *American Economic Review, Papers and Proceedings*, Vol. 81 (May 1991), pp. 222–26.

Froot, Kenneth A., "Japanese Foreign Direct Investment," NBER Working Paper 3737 (Cambridge, Massachusetts: National Bureau of Economic Research, June 1991).

Froot, Kenneth A., and Jeremy C. Stein, "Exchange Rates and Foreign Direct Investment: An Imperfect Capital Markets Approach," *Quarterly Journal of Economics*, Vol. 106 (November 1991), pp. 1191–1217.

Georgiou, George C., and Sharon Weinhold, "Japanese Direct Investment in the U.S.," *World Economy*, Vol. 15 (November 1992), pp. 761–78.

Graham, Edward M., and Paul R. Krugman, *Foreign Direct Investment in the United States*, 2nd ed. (Washington: Institute for International Economics, 1991).

Healey, Derek T., *Japanese Capital Exports and Asian Economic Development* (Paris: Development Centre of the OECD, 1991).

Heitger, Bernhard, and Jürgen Stehn, "Japanese Direct Investment in the EC—Response to the Internal Market 1992?" *Journal of Common Market Studies*, Vol. 29 (September 1990), pp. 1–15.

Hennart, J.-F., and Y.-R. Park, "Location, Governance, and Strategic Determinants of Japanese Manufacturing Investment in the United States," Working Paper (Champaign: University of Illinois, 1991).

International Monetary Fund, *Report on the Measurement of International Capital Flows* (Washington, 1992).

Iwamoto, Yasushi, "Japanese Corporate Tax Policy and Direct Investment Abroad," Australian National University Working Papers in Economics and Econometrics, No. 204 (Canberra, May 1990).

Japan Research Institute, "Research Study on Influences of Growing Foreign Direct Investments on International Structure of Industry and Trade," English summary (1990).

Jones, Ronald W., and J. Peter Neary, "The Positive Theory of International Trade," in *International Trade: Surveys of Theory and Policy*, edited by Ronald W. Jones (Amsterdam and New York: North-Holland, 1986).

Kawai, Masahiro, "Japanese Investment in Foreign Securities in the 1980s," Department of Economics Discussion Paper 91–37 (Vancouver: University of British Columbia, September 1991).

Kogut, Bruce, and Sea Jin Chang, "Technological Capabilities and Japanese Foreign Direct Investment in the United States," *Review of Economics and Statistics*, Vol. 73 (August 1991), pp. 401–13.

Kojima, Kiyoshi, and Terutomo Ozawa, "Micro- and Macroeconomic Models of Direct Investment: Toward a Synthesis," *Hitotsubashi Journal of Economics*, Vol. 25 (June 1984), pp. 1–20.

Komiya, Ryutaro, and Ryuhei Wakasugi, "Japan's Foreign Direct Investment," *Annals of the American Academy of Political and Social Science*, Vol. 513 (January 1991), pp. 48–61.

Lizondo, J. Saul, "Foreign Direct Investment," in International Monetary Fund, *Determinants and Systemic Consequences of International Capital Flows*, Occasional Paper 77 (Washington, March 1991), pp. 68–82.

Mann, Catherine L., "Determinants of Japanese Direct Investment in U.S. Manufacturing Industries," *Journal of International Money and Finance*, Vol. 12 (October 1993), pp. 523–41.

Mundell, Robert A., "International Trade and Factor Mobility," *American Economic Review*, Vol. 47 (1957), pp. 321–35.

Nicolaides, Phedon, "Investment Policies in an Integrated World Economy," *World Economy*, Vol. 14 (June 1991), pp. 121–37.

Nicolaides, Phedon, and Stephen Thomsen, "Can Protectionism Explain Direct Investment," *Journal of Common Market Studies*, Vol. 29 (December 1991), pp. 635–43.

Sleuwaegen, Leo, "Foreign Direct Investment and Intra-Firm Trade: Evidence From Japan," Institute for Economic Research Discussion Paper 9002-G (Rotterdam: Erasmus Universiteit, 1990).

Tabata, Naoki, "Japanese Banks' Direct Investment to the United States," in JCIF Policy Study Series, No. 16 (Tokyo: Japan Center for International Finance, 1990), pp. 25–34.

Thomsen, Stephen, "Japanese Direct Investment in the European Community: The Product Cycle Revisited," *World Economy*, Vol. 16 (May 1993), pp. 301–15.

United Nations, Centre on Transnational Corporations, *The Determinants of Foreign Direct Investment: A Survey of the Evidence*, ST/CTC/121 (New York, 1992).

IV Demographic Change and Household Saving in Japan

Guy Meredith

Demographic projections for coming decades indicate that, of the major industrial countries, Japan will experience the most rapid increase in the share of the elderly in the total population.[1] This demographic shift is expected to cause pressures on the financing of the social security system and slower growth in the labor force and in potential output. Many observers also believe that a consequence of the transition to a more elderly population will be a reduction in the private saving rate, based on the view that retired households save less than those of working age. Such a decline would reduce the flow of saving to both Japan and overseas economies, implying a reduction in domestic investment or the external surplus, or both.

The view that the transition to a more elderly population will reduce the aggregate saving rate is controversial, however. Broadly speaking, there are two schools of thought on the issue of saving and demographics. The first, associated with the life-cycle model of household behavior, views saving as being motivated by the desire of households to smooth lifetime consumption in the face of uneven income flows. The saving rate of the working-age population is positive, whereas that of the retired population is negative. An increase in the ratio of the retired population to the working-age population thus lowers the aggregate saving rate. The second view follows from evidence suggesting that the saving rate of the elderly is not significantly lower than that of the overall population, a phenomenon that is sometimes attributed to the existence of an altruistic bequest motive for saving. An inference drawn from the apparent similarity of saving rates of different age groups is that a shift toward a more elderly population will have little effect on the aggregate saving rate.

This section first reviews the literature on demographics and saving, with a focus on the Japanese experience. As shown in the next part, the aggregate evidence on saving and demographic structure for Japan and other countries appears to be consistent with the life-cycle model. Some studies using household data, however, seem to contradict predictions of the life-cycle model. In the third part, the household data for Japan are re-examined. These data show that retired households in Japan do, in fact, dissave; the rate of dissaving is magnified when income is adjusted for social security benefits. Indeed, it appears that an inappropriate treatment of social security and pension income is a flaw in many household-level studies, both for Japan and other countries. The fourth part presents simulation results, based on a life-cycle model, that suggest that Japan's private saving rate will decline significantly as a result of demographic factors. The last part summarizes the results.

Previous Studies on Demographics and Saving

Evidence Supporting the Life-Cycle Model

Much work has been done on the ability of the life-cycle model to explain aggregate saving.[2] As discussed above, an important prediction of the model is that a shift in the demographic structure toward a higher ratio of elderly households to working-age households will reduce the aggregate saving rate. In addition, life-cycle models that include a period of youth preceding working life predict that the aggregate saving rate will be negatively related to the population share of the young. Another prediction of the life-cycle model is that saving during working life will depend on expected income from sources other than household saving during retirement. For instance, income in the form of benefits from fully funded private pension plans is likely to reduce saving by working-age households, excluding contributions to pension plans. Unfunded public pension plans also tend to reduce household saving in a life-cycle model, although the exact impact is complicated by the implicit rate of return households expect to realize on their contributions and the possible earnings-testing of benefits.[3]

---

[1] A comparison of the outlook for the major industrial countries is presented in Masson and Tryon (1990).

[2] For one of the early expositions of the life-cycle model, see Ando and Modigliani (1963).

[3] When pension benefits are lump sum and the expected return on contributions equals the market interest rate, the offset will be one for one. When benefits are earnings-tested, or the rate of return exceeds the market interest rate, social security may induce households to retire earlier. Higher private saving for a longer retirement period (the "retirement" effect) would then tend to offset, at least partially, the saving "replacement" effect (see Feldstein (1974)).

Table 4-1. Summary of Studies on Demographics and Saving

	Data Source	Effect on Saving Rate of 1 Percentage Point Rise in Demographic Ratio	
		Youth[1]	Elderly[2]
Aggregate cross-section studies			
1. Modigliani (1970)	...	−0.20 (3.7)	−0.88 (3.1)
2. Modigliani and Sterling (1983)	...	−0.13 (1.4)	−0.51 (4.3)
3. Feldstein (1980)	...	−0.77 (3.9)	−1.21 (2.7)
4. Horioka (1986)	21 OECD countries 1976–82 average	−0.92 (4.2)	−1.61 (4.0)
5. Graham (1987)	24 OECD countries, 1975 or 1970–80 average	−0.87 (2.9)	0.12 (0.3)
6. Koskela and Viren (1989)	23 countries, 1979–83 average	−0.73 (1.7)	−0.76 (0.8)
7. Horioka (1991)	21 OECD countries	−0.44 (1.7)	−1.09 (2.4)
8. OECD (1990)	14 OECD countries, 1980–88 average	...	−0.93 (2.4)
Time-series studies			
9. Shibuya (1987)	1966–83 (Japan)	...	−0.34 (3.8)
10. Horioka (1991)	1956–87 (Japan)	−0.30 (5.1)	−1.13 (3.7)
11. Masson and Tryon (1990)	1969–87 pooled[3]	−1.10	−1.10
Average estimated impact	—	**−0.61**	**−0.86**

Note: Lines 1, 2, and 3 are cited in Heller (1989); line 5 is from Graham's equation 1 in Table 2; line 6 is from Koskela and Viren's equation (6) in Table 1; lines 7 and 10 are cited in Horioka (1991); line 9 is a simulated effect based on 1980 values; line 11 is the simulated post-1980 impact. Figures in parentheses are estimated t-statistics.
[1]Ratio of population aged 0–19 to population aged 20–64.
[2]Ratio of population over 64 to population aged 20–64, except line 8 is ratio to total population.
[3]Pooled data for the seven major industrial countries and the small industrial countries.

Evidence based on aggregate data typically supports the predictions of the life-cycle model regarding demographics and saving, as indicated by the results shown in Table 4-1. Most of the studies have been based on cross-section data for OECD countries, while others have used time-series data for Japan only or have pooled cross-section and time-series data for several industrial countries. The methodology typically has involved regressing the saving rate on variables that capture the demographic structure of the population and other factors. The demographic structure is summarized by the ratios of the elderly and the young to the population of working age—that is, the elderly and youth dependency ratios.

In most cases, the demographic effects are both statistically and economically significant. The impact of a change in the elderly dependency ratio typically exceeds that of the youth dependency ratio: an unweighted average of the estimation results indicates that a 1 percentage point rise in the elderly ratio lowers the saving rate by 0.86 percentage point, whereas the same increase in the youth dependency ratio lowers the saving rate by 0.61 percentage point. Effects of this magnitude imply a large change in the aggregate saving rate in response to projected shifts in Japan's demographic structure. Specifically, the elderly dependency ratio is projected to rise by over 20 percentage points from the first half of the

1990s to 2020. In the absence of changes in other factors that affect saving, these results would suggest a reduction in the household saving rate of over 15 percentage points.[4]

Fewer studies have examined the impact of social security on private saving in Japan. Using aggregate time-series data from the period 1966–83, Shibuya (1987) found a significant negative effect from the social security replacement ratio. Yamada, Yamada, and Liu (1990) also found a significant effect of social security retirement benefits on both the saving and retirement decisions, using time-series data for the 1951–82 period. The saving replacement effect dominates the retirement effect, leading to a strong negative overall impact on saving from the introduction of the social security system.

Challenges to the Life-Cycle Model

Other studies have cast doubt on the applicability of the life-cycle model for both Japan and other countries, on the basis of the observed saving behavior of the elderly in household data. In particular, these studies suggest that the saving rates of elderly households are not significantly lower than those of working-age households; that the elderly do not decumulate assets; and that elderly households leave substantial bequests. Hayashi, Ando, and Ferris (1988), for instance, found only limited support for the life-cycle model in the behavior of elderly single-member households in Japan. For the elderly more generally, they attributed the apparent lack of wealth decumulation to the importance of intergenerational bequests. Bosworth, Burtless, and Sabelhaus (1991) attempted to infer the effect of demographic changes on Japan's aggregate saving rate by examining differences in age-specific saving rates. In particular, they held the saving rate of each age group constant and changed the population shares of each group to obtain alternative aggregate saving rates.[5] The size of the effect on the aggregate saving rate depended on how different the age-specific saving rates were; these authors concluded that the differences in saving rates were not large enough to affect the aggregate saving rate (Bosworth, Burtless, and Sabelhaus (1991, pp. 220–21)).

The (apparent) high saving rate of the elderly has sometimes been explained in terms of a dynastic model of household behavior, in which the current generation cares about the welfare of the next generation (see Barro (1974)). Such intergenerational altruism can motivate intentional bequests, explaining why the propensity of elderly households to consume out of wealth might be lower than that predicted by the life-cycle model. However, although the dynastic model can explain intentional bequests, it is less clear that it can explain why the saving rates of elderly households would be similar to those of working-age households.[6] In particular, in both the dynastic and life-cycle models, households will smooth consumption over time. If income is not similarly smooth, then the household saving rate will vary systematically with income in either framework. Continued saving by the elderly, then, must imply that their incomes do not decline with age.[7] This is not a prediction of either the life-cycle or dynastic model per se, but rather must reflect either continued high labor supply by elderly households, or the replacement of labor income by other sources of income as households age. These issues are examined in the next part of this section.

Measurement of Saving in Household Data

There are two difficulties with studies of household saving that show continued saving by the elderly. The first is that income and wealth are often defined inappropriately, in that no distinction is made between earned income and other sources of income. The second is that household saving is often not observed directly; rather, saving is inferred from hypothetically constructed wealth profiles of the elderly, and these profiles may be subject to considerable mismeasurement.

As regards the definitions of income and wealth, it is important to distinguish between earned income and income from other sources such as social security benefits and private pension plans. The former yields a flow of goods and services to the economy as a whole, while the latter represents either a transfer from other households or the running down of assets that are not included in household balance sheets. Income from fully funded private pension plans is an example of retirement income that largely represents asset decumulation.[8] Benefits from a pay-as-you-go social security program represent transfers from working-age to retired households—consumption out of this income will lower the saving rate for the economy as a whole, unless consumption by working-age households falls by an equivalent amount. This will

---

[4] Horioka (1991) has presented calculations that yield even larger effects, implying that the household saving rate would become significantly negative as early as 2010.

[5] Appendix 4-1 provides an example of why holding the saving rates of different age groups constant is inappropriate in the presence of a social security program that is not fully funded.

[6] See Auerbach, Cai, and Kotlikoff (1990) for a dynastic model that generates significant changes in saving rates as a result of demographic transitions.

[7] Imperfections in capital markets could limit the ability of households to smooth consumption by borrowing against future earnings. To the extent that such constraints are relevant in the life-cycle model, consumption would tend to be lower in the early stages of life and higher in the retirement period. This would tend to magnify the gap between the saving rates of working-age and elderly households.

[8] Interest income on the remaining principal is small relative to the rate at which the principal is being run down.

not, in general, be the case when households are forward looking. As illustrated in Appendix 4-1, working-age households will spread the effect of a change in social security taxes over both current and future consumption. A rise in transfers from the young to the elderly then reduces the consumption of the young by less than it increases that of the elderly, causing the aggregate saving rate to fall.

The second difficulty with some household studies is that they must infer, only on the basis of observations for a single period of the wealth of households of different ages, how the wealth of households will change over time.[9] There are several reasons why this is problematic, especially in the case of Japan. One is that the elderly poor tend to get absorbed in the families of their children and thus drop out of the sample of households. Looking, in a given year, at the profile of household wealth by age of the household head then tends to overrepresent relatively rich elderly households. Bias also arises because the elderly who have been hospitalized on a long-term basis are not included in survey data. Their saving rates are typically very negative, especially when the public health care component of their consumption is included. Furthermore, adjustments must be made because households of different ages have different lifetime incomes and, thus, asset wealth owing to productivity growth and other factors. Although researchers typically attempt to control for these "cohort" effects, the techniques are often arbitrary. In general, the power of the results is weakened by the need to impute key information.[10] Finally, the translation of wealth profiles into saving rates is complicated by unanticipated capital gains and losses on existing wealth, as well as inter vivos transfers.

The problems of adjusting for unearned income and imputing wealth profiles can be avoided by using direct information on the consumption and income by source of elderly households. This permits the distinction between earned and unearned income and obviates the need to construct artificial age-wealth profiles. Such data were compiled in Japan for both retired and working elderly households in the 1990 *Annual Report on the Family Income and Expenditure Survey* (FIES; Japan (1990)), as shown in Table 4-2.

Elderly retired households in Japan account for 11½ percent of the total households covered in the survey, whereas elderly working households account for 5 percent.[11] For retired households, living expenditures exceed disposable income by a significant margin: on average,

these households *dissave* at an annual rate of 21 percent, even before adjusting for unearned income. In the event, unearned income in the form of social security benefits accounts for by far the largest component of income for retired households, averaging over 70 percent of total income.[12] For elderly households whose head is still working (whose average age is significantly lower than that for retired households), the situation is quite different: the saving rate remains positive at 17½ percent— income is almost double that of retired households, while expenditures are only 30 percent higher. These data suggest that, after retirement, household income drops off more sharply than consumption, resulting in dissaving for retired households.[13] The drop in earned income, however, is partially buffered by a rise in transfer payments, and this moderates the change in the saving rate that would otherwise be observed.

The aggregate saving rate of both retired and working elderly households is minus 3½ percent, compared with the 25 percent saving rate of working-age households computed from the 1990 FIES. Assuming that the saving rates of these two groups remain unchanged, it is possible to calculate the effect of a shift in the demographic structure toward a higher proportion of elderly. Specifically, a rise in the elderly dependency ratio of 1 percentage point would lower the aggregate saving rate by 0.2 percentage point, holding the saving rate of elderly and working-age households constant.[14] While significant in light of the size of the projected rise in the elderly dependency ratio, this response is substantially lower than the average estimated effect obtained using aggregate data shown in Table 4-1. The difference is examined in more detail in the next part of this section.

Simulation Using a Life-Cycle Model

It was shown above that there are significant differences in the saving rates of elderly and working-age households in Japan. Nevertheless, holding the saving rate of each group constant, the impact of a demographic shift on the aggregate saving rate is smaller than that suggested by some econometric studies. A more sophisticated estimate of the effect of demographic shifts on aggregate saving is presented below. Specifically, a life-cycle model for Japan is simulated using projected changes in the age composition of the population. The

---

[9] This is especially true for the United States, where insufficient data have been available on household consumption to observe household saving rates directly.

[10] Campbell (1991), for instance, has questioned the approach taken by Hayashi and others (1988).

[11] Elderly households are defined as having a household head aged 60 years or over.

[12] Takayama (1992) observes a similarly high ratio of social security benefits to household income in the 1984 *National Survey of Family Income and Expenditures*.

[13] These data are only suggestive because of possible differences in the characteristics of working and retired households.

[14] The initial elderly dependency ratio is 19 percent, and the ratio of the disposable income of working-age to elderly households is 1.8.

Table 4-2. Income, Consumption, and Saving of Retired Households[1]
(Monthly average in thousands of yen)

	1988	1989	1990
Household income	201.5	209.0	225.5
Taxes	24.0	23.7	24.4
Tax rate (in percent)	11.9	11.3	10.8
Disposable income	177.4	185.3	202.8
Wages and salaries	27.8	32.4	31.5
Business and homework	4.0	4.6	4.5
Social security benefits	143.0	143.9	165.9[2]
Other	14.2	14.0	12.1
Disposable income excluding social security benefits ("earned" income)	51.4	57.7	54.8
Living expenditures	212.9	220.2	228.3
Saving rates			
Total saving rate (in percent)[3]	−20.0	−18.8	−12.6
Saving rate as a ratio to earned income[4]	−314.2	−281.6	−316.6
Ratio of earned income to total household living expenditures	24.1	26.2	24.0

Source: Japan, Management and Coordination Agency (1990, Table 18, p. 114).
[1]Defined as households whose head is jobless and over age 60.
[2]The surge in 1990 is due to a reduction in the payment interval for annuity benefits from three to two months.
[3]Defined as disposable income less living expenditures as a share of disposable income.
[4]Saving rate out of disposable income, excluding social security benefits.

results indicate an effect on saving exceeding that suggested by differences in household saving rates, but lower than the average estimate obtained using aggregate data.

The life-cycle model is described in detail in Appendix 4-2. It follows in the tradition of Tobin (1967) and White (1978), in that the focus is on the behavior of individual households, with variables such as the real interest rate and the real growth rate held to be exogenous. The representative household is forward looking and maximizes lifetime utility subject to a budget constraint. Household income consists of after-tax labor income, interest income on accumulated assets, social security benefits, and inherited wealth. The consumption path is affected by factors such as the rate of time preference, the real interest rate, and the intertemporal elasticity of substitution. Uncertainty about the time of death causes households to plan to consume less toward the end of their life span, reflecting a lower probability that they will be alive to benefit from this consumption.[15] Uncertainty about death also gener-

ates a precautionary demand for saving. Because wealth cannot become negative even if the household lives beyond the average life expectancy, households plan to finance consumption over a longer life span than they expect, on average, to live. This implies that households typically die with positive wealth and leave bequests to the next generation, even though they derive no utility from bequests per se.

Initial values for certain variables were chosen to be consistent with observed data for Japan during the 1970–90 period: in particular, the risk-free real interest rate averaged 3 percent;[16] labor-augmented productivity growth averaged 1¾ percent; and population growth averaged 1 percent. Parameters determining consumption profiles were similar to those used in other studies of household behavior.[17] Simulating the model with these assumptions yielded a household saving rate of 16.7 per-

[15] See Hurd (1990) for a discussion of the effect of mortality hazard on consumption profiles.

[16] As measured by the ex post yield on government bonds, adjusted for increases in the GNP deflator.

[17] The parameterization of the model is discussed in more detail in Appendix 4-2.

cent and a ratio of household assets to income (that is, accumulated wealth) of 5.5, compared with observed data (1970–90 average) of 18.0 percent and 5.5, respectively.

The predictions of the model are very similar to the actual data, both for the saving rate and the level of accumulated assets. The appropriateness of the life-cycle model was also tested by comparing its predictions for the behavior of elderly households with the observed data. The household survey data obtained from the 1990 FIES were first corrected for imputed rent on owner-occupied housing by multiplying the estimated value of owner-occupied housing by the rate of return on other assets in the model. This imputed rent was added to both the observed income and consumption of elderly households, and the saving rate was recalculated on a consistent basis. For elderly households in 1990, the model's prediction for the saving rate was −2 percent compared with an adjusted observed saving rate of −2½ percent. Predictions for the share in income of earned income, social security benefits, and other income were 31, 34, and 35 percent, respectively, compared with adjusted survey data of 30, 32, and 38 percent. Again, the predicted and actual series correspond closely. The consistency of the predictions with the observed data is reassuring evidence that the life-cycle model can provide a realistic characterization of household saving behavior.[18]

The model was then simulated to track projected demographic changes over the period 1990–2030. The elderly dependency ratio is projected to rise from 17.7 in 1990 to 46.2 in 2030. The model results for the projected household saving rate were: 1990, 21.3 percent; 2000, 18.7 percent; 2010, 14.7 percent; 2020, 12.0 percent; 2030, 10.4 percent—implying a total change during the 1990–2030 period of −10.9 percent. Of course, this simulation indicates only the change in the household saving rate attributable to demographic considerations; the actual change in the saving rate will depend on other factors. For instance, the decline in saving would tend to be moderated by a rise in the real interest rate if lower saving otherwise would cause a shortage of saving relative to investment.[19]

The ratio of the simulated change in the household saving rate to the change in the elderly dependency ratio over the 1990–2030 period is about 0.4. This lies between the estimates discussed above: specifically, the ratio of 0.2 obtained by changing population shares while holding the saving rates of the elderly and the working-age populations constant; and the average estimated impact of 0.86 derived from aggregate data.

The difference between the simulation results and the impact when household saving rates are held unchanged is due primarily to the induced effect on the saving rates of changes in social security taxes. In particular, social security tax rates are currently low relative to those that will be needed to support a higher ratio of elderly to working-age households in the future (see Section V of this volume). As illustrated in Appendix 4-1, the increase in the tax rate will be reflected partly in lower consumption of working-age households, and partly in a reduction in their saving rate. This induced effect on the saving rate of working households reinforces that of the shift in weights toward elderly households with a lower saving rate.

It is more difficult to reconcile the predictions of the life-cycle model with the estimation results obtained using aggregate data. One possibility is that the household data on which the life-cycle model is based may underrepresent some elderly households that have high rates of dissaving, such as those in which the head of the household is hospitalized. In this case, the picture provided by the aggregate data would be more accurate. However, estimation using aggregate data has yielded a considerable range of estimates. The lack of consensus reflects, in part, that differences in the population structure across time periods and countries tend to be correlated with other macroeconomic variables. The comovement in these variables makes the estimation results sensitive to the exact specification of the equations and can lead to "overfitting" the data.[20] In any event, it is interesting that the effect predicted by the life-cycle model is quite close to that obtained in the only study based exclusively on aggregate Japanese data since the mid-1960s (Shibuya (1987)).

Conclusions

This paper has analyzed the probable effect on the household saving rate of a shift in Japan's demographic structure toward a more elderly population. Although many econometric studies using aggregate data have predicted a very large effect on the saving rate, some studies using household data suggest that the impact may be small.

By using more recent and detailed information on the income and consumption of retired households, the analysis has shown that the saving rates for the elderly

---

[18] This evidence supports the original findings of Tobin (1967) for the United States and contradicts those of White (1978) and other authors who have suggested that the life-cycle model is not capable of explaining observed household saving behavior.

[19] The saving rate would also be affected by the stance of fiscal policy. These simulations assume that the pension system is operated on a pay-as-you-go basis, implying a future rise in contribution rates to balance increasing benefits. Section V of this volume discusses alternative long-run simulations in more detail.

[20] The collinearity of the explanatory variables implies that t-statistics may be low, even though the parameters are large in absolute magnitude. The choice of a specification that yields statistically significant parameters may imply parameter values that lie on the high end of the range of values that would be supported by the data.

calculated in some household-level studies may be misleading. It appears that the elderly *do* dissave, and that the rate of dissaving is very similar to that predicted by a life-cycle model of household behavior. In addition, a large share of the income of the retired elderly in Japan consists of social security benefits, which represent transfer payments from the working generation as opposed to a net flow of resources to the economy. The existence of social security benefits and taxes implies that the effect on the aggregate saving rate of changes in population shares cannot be assessed by holding the saving rates of elderly and working-age households constant.

Simulations of a life-cycle model indicate that the household saving rate is likely to decline steadily in coming decades as a result of the shift toward a more elderly population. Although the effect of this demographic shift is significant, it is smaller than that suggested by some studies using aggregate data, which have suggested that the household saving rate may become *negative* over the long run. The effect is larger, however, than the change implied when the saving rates of the elderly and working-age populations are held constant, because of the role played by social security benefits and taxes.

Appendix 4-1. Effects of Demographic Change on Saving With and Without Social Security

In simple versions of the life-cycle model, the saving rate of each generation is independent and unaffected by the demographic structure of the population. The effect of a demographic transition on the aggregate saving rate then equals the change in the share of each generation in total income multiplied by its saving rate:

$$\Delta(S/Y) = \Sigma \ \Delta w_i s_i \ , \qquad (A4\text{-}1)$$

where Δw_i is the change in the share of generation i in aggregate income, and s_i is its saving rate. Demographic shifts alter w_i and thus the aggregate saving rate when s_i differs across generations. This decomposition is not useful, however, when the income of some generation is zero because s_i is undefined. An alternative approach that avoids this problem defines saving as a share of consumption:

$$\Delta(S/C) = \Sigma \ \Delta w_i' s_i' \ , \qquad (A4\text{-}2)$$

where $\Delta w_i'$ and s_i' refer, respectively, to the share of each generation in aggregate consumption and its saving-to-consumption ratio.

A simple example of the effect of a demographic transition without social security is shown in the upper panel of Table 4-3. Each household divides its consumption equally between two periods; household income equals 1 in the first period and 0 in the second; the interest rate is 0. In the initial equilibrium—period 1—it is assumed that there are one "young" household and one "elderly" household. The aggregate wealth of the economy is ½, representing the saving of the young to finance consumption in retirement. The saving rate of the young in relation to consumption is 1, while that of the elderly is −1. The aggregate saving rate is 0, since each generation has an equal share in total consumption.

In period 2, the demographic structure shifts as the number of young households rises to two while the number of elderly households remains at one. Wealth rises, and the economy-wide saving rate becomes positive. The change in the latter can be inferred from equation (A4-2), since the share of the young in total consumption rises to ⅔. In period 3, the number of young households returns to one, while there are now two elderly households. Economy-wide saving is negative because the wealth accumulated in period 2 is consumed by the elderly households. In period 4, the demographic transition is complete: saving and wealth have returned to their initial levels. An important aspect of this example is that, in each period, the saving-to-consumption ratio of the two generations is unchanged at 1 for the young and −1 for the elderly. This allows the effect on the aggregate saving rate of demographic shifts to be calculated using the above decomposition combined with unchanged saving rates.

Calculating the effect of a demographic transition is more complex in the presence of an unfunded social security program. In this case, the tax burden on young households depends on the number of elderly households that must be supported. Changes in the tax burden affect the saving decision of young households, leading to an interdependence between their saving rate and the demographic structure. This is illustrated in the lower panel of Table 4-3. The demographic transition is the same as in the first example; now, however, a social security program transfers income of ½ to each elderly household. These transfers are financed on a pay-as-you-go basis by taxes on young households. The initial equilibrium in period 1 is the same as that described above, except that young households do not save because consumption during retirement is financed by social security benefits. This lowers aggregate wealth to 0. In period 2, the social security tax rate on young households falls because the ratio of young to elderly households rises. Young households save a part of this tax cut to finance consumption during retirement; thus, their saving rate becomes positive, and economy-wide saving also becomes positive.

In period 3, the tax rate on the young households rises sharply to finance social security benefits for elderly households. The saving rates of both generations become negative because the elderly consume wealth accumulated in period 2, while the young finance a part of their social security taxes by going into debt. In period 4, the demographic structure returns to the initial equilibrium, but the saving rate is raised because of previous demographic changes. This "echo" effect occurs because the

Table 4-3. Effect of a Demographic Transition on Aggregate Saving

	Period 1			Period 2			Period 3			Period 4		
	Young	Old	Total	Young	Old	Total	Young	Old	Total	Young	Old	Total
Population	1	1	2	2	1	3	1	2	3	1	1	1
						Without social security						
Consumption	½	½	1	1	½	1½	½	1	1½	½	½	1
Income	1	0	1	2	0	2	1	0	1	1	0	1
Wealth (end of period)	½	0	½	1	0	1	½	0	½	½	0	½
Saving	½	−½	0	1	−½	½	½	−1	−½	½	−½	0
Saving/income	½	—	0	½	—	¼	½	—	−½	½	—	0
Saving/consumption	1	−1	0	1	−1	⅓	1	−1	−⅓	1	−1	0
						With unfunded social security program						
Consumption	½	½	1	1¼	½	1¾	¼	1¼	1½	½	¼	¾
Income												
Earned	1	0	1	2	0	2	1	0	1	1	0	1
Social security	−½	½	0	−½	½	0	−1	1	0	−½	½	0
Total	½	½	1	1½	½	2	0	1	1	½	½	1
Wealth (end of period)	0	0	0	¼	0	¼	−¼	0	−¼	0	0	0
Saving	0	0	0	¼	0	¼	−¼	−¼	−½	0	¼	¼
Saving/total income	0	0	0	⅙	0	⅛	—	−¼	−½	0	½	¼
Saving/consumption	0	0	0	⅕	0	1/7	−1	−⅕	−⅓	0	1	⅓

elderly household must save out of social security benefits to repay debt incurred in period 3. Period 5 (not shown in the table) is identical to period 1—both wealth and saving are 0.

Although this example is very stylized, it indicates some important aspects of the effect of demographic change on saving in the presence of an unfunded social security program. The first is that the saving rates of the young and elderly vary over time in response to demographic shifts. This means that the approach of weighting fixed saving rates by changing population shares is invalid. For instance, in period 1, the saving rates of both generations are zero. Varying the weights applied to these saving rates would imply—incorrectly—an unchanged aggregate saving rate in the face of a demographic shift. The second point is that there is no general tendency for the saving rate of the young to exceed that of the elderly. Indeed, in periods 3 and 4, the saving rate of elderly households *exceeds* that of young households. Nevertheless, the shift toward a more elderly population in period 3 reduces the aggregate saving rate by the same amount as in the example in which there is no social security and the saving rate of the elderly is always below that of the young.

Appendix 4-2. A Life-Cycle Model of Household Behavior for Japan

The life-cycle model used in this section is similar to that described by Tobin (1967) for the United States. The principal differences are that the model used here takes into account social security benefits and contributions, and also allows for precautionary saving, since the risk of death is not insured through private annuity contracts. In addition, the model used here is solved numerically rather than analytically, allowing more general specification of some relationships. The economy consists of overlapping generations of households, each of whose behavior follows life-cycle principles. A period in the model is one year in length. Households are assumed to become economically active at age 20, and the oldest possible age is 100. Each life-cycle then consists of 81 periods, and there are 81 distinct ages of households living at any time.

The time of death is uncertain; the probability of dying at a given age is based on 1990 mortality tables for Japan. Households maximize expected lifetime utility subject to the constraint that they cannot die with negative wealth even if they live to the oldest possible age. Thus the present value of planned consumption to age 100 cannot exceed that of lifetime wealth. Households that die *before* age 100 typically die with positive assets and leave a bequest; the after-tax value of bequests is divided among households aged 20 (the effective tax rate on bequests is assumed to be 25 percent).

Household wealth at age 20 consists of human wealth, social security wealth, and bequests. Human wealth is the discounted value of labor income, based on a cross-section profile of household labor income from the 1990 FIES. The profile of labor income shifts up over time, on the basis of assumed productivity growth of 1.7 percent a year. Growth in the earnings of a specific household then reflects both movements up the age-earnings profile as well as the upward trend in the profile itself. Households pay social security taxes on labor income and receive benefits beginning at age 60, on the basis of an average replacement rate of 40 percent. The tax rate on workers is adjusted to finance benefits on a pay-as-you-go basis. Labor supply is exogenous; thus, labor income is not affected by changes in the social security tax rate or benefits.

The consumption path of each household is determined by maximizing lifetime utility, where the latter is defined as the utility of "discretionary" consumption in each period discounted by a rate of time preference (ρ); the rate of time preference was set to equal 0 in the simulations, following Tobin (1967). The utility derived from discretionary consumption is proportional to the number of "adult-equivalent" members of the household at a given time; for this purpose, each child under the age of 20 represents ½ of an adult. The utility function for each period exhibits constant relative risk aversion; assuming a degree of risk aversion of unity implies that utility is simply the natural logarithm of consumption. Discretionary consumption at age t is measured as total consumption, C_t, less a minimum ("subsistence") level of consumption, $\overline{C}$:

$$U(C_t) = \log (C_t - \overline{C}).$$

The subsistence level of consumption was set to equal about ⅓ of the total consumption of working-age households. The optimal growth rate of discretionary consumption at age t is then

$$(C_t - \overline{C})/(C_{t-1} - \overline{C}) = \{ (1 + r)/[(1 + \rho)(1 + \alpha_t)] \},$$

where r is the real interest rate (assumed to remain constant at 3 percent a year), and α_t is the mortality hazard at age t. Household saving in each period equals the difference between income and consumption, where income includes the return on accumulated assets.

The equilibrium household saving rate and assets-to-income ratio for an assumed population growth rate of 1 percent a year were shown in the main text. The effect on the results of changing the population and productivity growth rates, and other parameters, was also examined. Compared with the baseline saving rate of 16.7 percent

and asset-to-income ratio of 5.5, when the population growth rate is raised to 2 percent a year, the saving rate rises to 17.2 percent, but the asset-income ratio falls to 4.3. If productivity growth is raised to 2.7 percent a year, the saving rate drops to 12.2 percent, and the asset-income ratio falls to 3.0. When the real interest rate is increased to 4 percent a year, the saving rate jumps to 20.1 percent, and the asset-income ratio rises to 6.7 compared with the baseline. Increasing the social security replacement rate by 10 percent, to 50 percent, makes the saving rate fall to 13.9 percent, and the asset-income ratio drops to 4.6.

The most notable aspect of these results is that the saving rate declines in response to higher productivity growth. In contrast, some proponents of the life-cycle model have maintained that the saving rate should depend *positively* on productivity growth because a faster growth rate would shift income to the working generation—who have high saving rates—thus raising the aggregate saving rate. Such a result, however, depends on the assumption that working-age households are not forward looking. When they *are* forward looking, faster productivity growth raises lifetime resources relative to current income, lowering the saving rate. This offsets the shift in income to working-age households: the net impact on savings is ambiguous a priori. In the model considered here, the rise in consumption by the young more than offsets the shift in income shares, causing the aggregate saving rate to fall.

References

Ando, Albert, and Franco Modigliani, "The Life Cycle Hypothesis of Savings," *American Economic Review*, Vol. 53 (May 1963), pp. 55–84.

Auerbach, Alan J., Jinyong Cai, and Laurence J. Kotlikoff, "U.S. Demographics and Saving: Predictions of Three Saving Models," NBER Working Paper 3404 (Cambridge, Massachusetts: National Bureau of Economic Research, July 1990).

Barro, Robert J., "Are Government Bonds Net Wealth?" *Journal of Public Economics*, Vol. 82 (November–December 1974), pp. 1095–1117.

Bosworth, Barry, Gary Burtless, and John Sabelhaus, "The Decline in Saving: Evidence from Household Surveys," *Brookings Papers on Economic Activity: 1* (1991), The Brookings Institution (Washington), pp. 183–256.

Campbell, David W., "Wealth Accumulation of the Elderly in Extended Families in Japan and the Distribution of Wealth Within Japanese Cohorts by Household Composition: A Critical Analysis of the Literature," Jerome Levy Economics Institute Working Paper 63 (New York: Bard College, September 1991).

Feldstein, Martin, "Social Security, Induced Retirement, and Aggregate Capital Accumulation," *Journal of Public Economics*, Vol. 82 (November–December 1974), pp. 905–26.

———, "International Differences in Social Security and Saving," *Journal of Public Economics*, Vol. 14 (October 1980), pp. 225–44.

Graham, J.W., "International Differences in Saving Rates and the Life Cycle Hypothesis," *European Economic Review*, Vol. 31 (1987), pp. 1509–29.

Hayashi, Fumio, Albert Ando, and R. Ferris, "Life Cycle and Bequest Savings," *Journal of the Japanese and International Economies*, Vol. 2 (December 1988), pp. 417–49.

Heller, Peter S., "Aging, Savings, and Pensions in the Group of Seven Countries: 1980–2025," *Journal of Public Policy*, Vol. 9 (April-June 1989), pp. 127–53.

Horioka, Charles Y., "Why Is Japan's Private Saving Rate So High?" (unpublished; Washington: International Monetary Fund, June 1986).

———, "The Determinants of Japan's Saving Rate: The Impact of the Age Structure of the Population and Other Factors," *Economic Studies Quarterly*, Vol. 42 (September 1991), pp. 237–53.

Hurd, Michael D., "Research on the Elderly: Economic Status, Retirement, and Consumption and Saving," *Journal of Economic Literature*, Vol. 28 (June 1990), pp. 565–637.

Japan, Management and Coordination Agency, *Annual Report on the Family Income and Expenditure Survey, 1990* (Tokyo: Office of the Prime Minister, Statistics Bureau, 1990).

Koskela, Erkki, and Matti Viren, "International Differences in Saving Rates and the Life Cycle Hypothesis: A Comment," *European Economic Review*, Vol. 33 (September 1989), pp. 1489–98.

Masson, Paul R., and Ralph W. Tryon, "Macroeconomic Effects of Population Aging in Industrial Countries," *Staff Papers* (IMF), Vol. 37 (September 1990), pp. 435–85.

Modigliani, Franco, "The Life Cycle Hypothesis of Saving and Intercountry Differences in the Saving Ratio," in *Induction, Growth, and Trade*, edited by W.A. Eltis, M.F. Scott, and J.N. Wolfe (Oxford: Clarendon, 1970), pp. 197–225.

Modigliani, Franco, and A. Sterling, "Determinants of Private Savings with Special Reference to the Role of Social Security—Cross-Country Tests," in *The Determinants of National Saving and Wealth*, edited by Franco Modigliani and Richard Hemming (New York: St. Martin's, 1983), pp. 24–55.

Organization for Economic Cooperation and Development, *OECD Economic Surveys: Japan, 1989/90* (Paris, 1990).

Shibuya, Hiroshi, "Japan's Household Saving Rate: An Application of the Life Cycle Hypothesis," IMF Working Paper 87/15 (Washington, March 1987).

Takayama, Noriyuki, *The Greying of Japan: An Economic Perspective on Public Pensions*, Economic Research Series, No. 30 (Tokyo: Institute of Economic Research, Hitotsubashi University, 1992).

Tobin, J., "Life Cycle Saving and Balanced Growth," in *Ten Studies in the Tradition of Irving Fisher*, edited by W. Fellner (New York: Wiley, 1967), pp. 231–56.

White, B.B., "Empirical Tests of the Life Cycle Hypothesis," *American Economic Review*, Vol. 68 (September 1978), pp. 546–60.

Yamada, Tetsuji, Tadashi Yamada, and Guoen Liu, "Determinants of Saving and Labor Force Participation of the Elderly in Japan," NBER Working Paper 3292 (Cambridge, Massachussetts: National Bureau of Economic Research, March 1990).

V Alternative Long-Run Scenarios

Guy Meredith

This section examines the long-run implications of an aging population for the Japanese economy. Demographic issues are of particular importance to Japan, given that the proportion of the elderly in the population will rise more rapidly over the next twenty-five years than in any other major industrial country.[1] Many observers have pointed to the surpluses in Japan's overall government balance prior to the recent economic downturn as indicating a fundamentally healthy fiscal position. Because the apparent health of Japan's fiscal position reflects large surpluses in the social security accounts, however, the implications of population aging for future social security receipts and payments are especially relevant. As shown below, the projected sharp future swing in the social security balance in the absence of measures to contain benefits and raise revenues underscores the need to take a forward-looking view of fiscal sustainability.

To summarize the results of simulations undertaken to explore various long-term scenarios, the increasing share of the elderly in the population will exert pressure for higher spending on both social security benefits and medical care. Under the structure of the social security program existing prior to the passage of reforms in late 1994, the ratio of pension benefits to GDP would rise from 5 percent of GDP in 1995 to 13 percent in 2020, and medical spending would rise by 2 percentage points of GDP.[2] In the absence of a compensating increase in pension contribution rates, the social security surplus would be eliminated shortly after the year 2000. Thereafter, rising benefits would lead to a primary social security *deficit* of 9 percent of GDP by 2020. Together with growing debt-servicing payments, unchanged policies would imply an overall government deficit of 16 percent of GDP by 2020, and a rise in net government debt to 150 percent of GDP.

To avoid such a debt explosion, actions must be taken to reform the pension system, and to cut general govern-

ment spending or raise revenues (or both). The magnitude of the adjustments needed to achieve a sustainable long-run fiscal position—defined as a stable ratio of debt to GDP—is estimated at 6½ percent of GDP if implemented in 1995. In other words, combined measures to raise revenues or reduce spending (or both) by this amount would be needed to put the fiscal position on a sustainable track. The longer the required adjustments are postponed, the larger they will ultimately need to be, given the intervening buildup in government debt.

The pension reform plan introduced in late 1994 envisages a phased-in rise in contribution rates, reduction in benefits, and postponement of the eligibility age. These steps will go far in addressing the fiscal imbalance. Even the full implementation over the next thirty years of these (ambitious) changes to the pension system would not be sufficient to put the fiscal position on a sustainable path, however. Further measures, totaling almost 2 percent of GDP if implemented in 1995, would be needed to fully offset the burden of the aging population. Of course, these conclusions are subject to the many provisos and uncertainties surrounding long-run projections. Nevertheless, the baseline projections provide strong warning signals about the future fiscal situation.

Population Dynamics and Output Growth

The upper panel of Chart 5-1 shows the magnitude of the rise in the old-age dependency ratio implied by the 1993 official population projections.[3] The ratio is pro-

---

[1] See, for instance, Van den Noord and Herd (1993).

[2] Long-run scenarios are subject to many uncertainties and provisos regarding, for instance, productivity growth and inflation. In Japan's case, however, over four fifths of all public pension benefits are ultimately indexed to wage growth, so different assumptions about economic growth would have little effect on the relative magnitude of future transfers to the elderly. In this case, the burden of an aging population depends more on the projected share of the elderly in the overall population, which is relatively robust to alternative demographic assumptions over the horizon considered here.

[3] These are based on the "middle series" published in 1993 by the Ministry of Health and Welfare. This projection assumes a recovery in Japan's fertility rate over the longer run to 1.8 births per woman from the current level of 1.5. If, instead, the fertility rate were to remain near the current level (as assumed in the Ministry's "low" projection), the rise in the old-age dependency ratio would be even larger, although most of the impact would be felt beyond the year 2020. Some analysts have expressed concern that even the "low" projection embodies too high a fertility rate, implying an even sharper rise in the old-age dependency ratio beyond about 2015. Beyond 2025, the fiscal position would worsen further because of continuing increases in the old-age dependency ratio. However, because these very long-term results are sensitive to demographic assumptions, the focus here is on the horizon over which the projected population structure is relatively robust to alternative assumptions.

Chart 5-1. Long-Term Demographic and Output Projections[1]

(In percent)

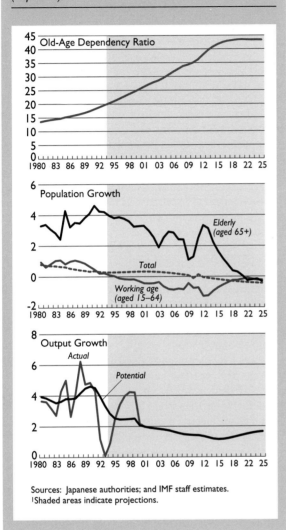

Sources: Japanese authorities; and IMF staff estimates.
[1]Shaded areas indicate projections.

jected to more than double, from 20 percent to almost 45 percent, during 1994–2020. Expressed as the ratio of the working population to the elderly, the number of people of working age for each elderly citizen will be more than halved, from 5 in 1995 to 2¼ by 2020. As shown in the middle panel, growth in the working-age population turns negative beyond 1995, with the pace of decline peaking at almost 1½ percent a year in 2015.

The bottom panel of Chart 5-1 illustrates the implications for Japan's potential output growth of slower growth in the working-age population. This projection is based on the assumptions that total factor productivity growth will continue at the rate expected for the 1990s; that the capital-to-output ratio will increase in line with the declining relative price of capital goods; and that the participation rate of the working-age population will be roughly constant beyond the year 2000. Under these assumptions, potential growth drops gradually from 2½ percent over the remainder of the 1990s, to about 1 percent in 2015, before recovering to about 1½ percent in 2025.

Alternative Fiscal Scenarios

The most important direct impact of population aging on the fiscal position will occur through a rise in social security benefits for the Employees' Pension Insurance Scheme (EPIS) and the National Pension Scheme (NPS). Benefits will increase in relation to GDP, not only because of the growing share of the elderly in the population, but also because of the maturation of Japan's pension scheme. Assuming that the key parameters determining pension benefits remained unchanged at their pre-reform levels—that is, eligibility at age 60 and full indexation to wage and price growth[4]—the ratio of benefits to GDP would rise from 5 percent in 1994 to 6¾ percent by 2000, and then to 13 percent by 2020. Another source of spending pressures will come from higher medical and health insurance payments, which are expected to rise by 2 percent of GDP during 1995–2020.[5]

Under the assumption of pre-reform program parameters, then, total spending on social security would rise from 12 percent of GDP in 1994 to 22½ percent in 2020 (Chart 5-2; upper panel). Social security contributions, meanwhile, would remain stable at 9½ percent of GDP.[6] The other components of government spending—current spending (excluding debt-servicing payments), public investment, and other revenues—are assumed to grow in line with nominal GDP. These developments would dramatically alter the overall fiscal position, as shown in the middle panel of Chart 5-2. The increase in social security benefits implies a swing in the primary social security balance of 10 percent of GDP from 1995 to 2020; including debt-servicing costs, the overall social security balance would shift from the current surplus of 3½ percent of GDP to a deficit of 12 percent. Adding to this the deficit on government operations excluding social security implies a rise in the overall deficit to 16 percent of GDP. The ratio of government debt to GDP grows slowly over the remainder of the 1990s and then accelerates sharply beyond 2000, rising to 150 percent of GDP by 2020.

These developments are clearly unsustainable, and significant measures must be taken to prevent an explosive rise in debt over the long run. An indication of the size

---

[4] Benefits under the EPIS are currently indexed to annual consumer price inflation, with a rebasing every five years to reflect the gap between average wage growth and inflation. NPS benefits are indexed to consumer price inflation.

[5] Based on updates to the estimates provided in Feldman (1985) using revised population projections.

[6] Excluding net transfers from the central Government and interest receipts.

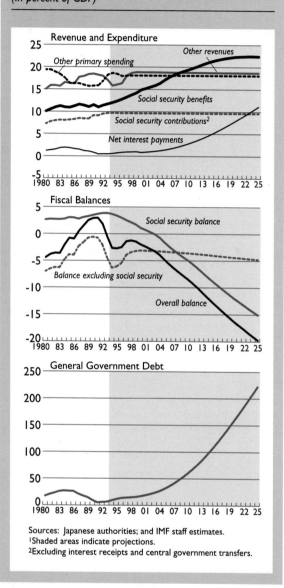

Chart 5-2. Long-Term Fiscal Projections: Pre-Reform Program Parameters[1]

(In percent of GDP)

Sources: Japanese authorities; and IMF staff estimates.
[1]Shaded areas indicate projections.
[2]Excluding interest receipts and central government transfers.

imbalance in the fiscal position, taking both current and future revenues and spending into account. Performing this exercise for Japan using the assumptions described above gives an imbalance of 6½ percent of GDP as of 1995. In other words, if the required adjustments were made in 1995, either a permanent increase in revenues of 6½ percent of GDP or a cut in expenditures of the same size (relative to the baseline scenario) would be needed to ensure that the debt stock does not rise without bound in the long run. If the adjustments are postponed, their ultimate size would need to be larger, since the debt stock and thus the debt-servicing burden would accumulate over the interval.[8]

To address the strains presented by population aging, the Ministry of Health and Welfare has introduced a package of reforms to the EPIS to be implemented in stages during 1995–2020.[9] There are three key elements to this package: (1) an increase in the combined employer/ employee contribution rate to the EPIS from the current 14½ percent of earnings to 29½ percent by 2020;[10] (2) a phased rise in the eligibility age for EPIS benefits from 60 to 65 starting in 2000; and (3) a shift to the use of "net" earnings—after payment of social security taxes— to index EPIS benefits. In addition, it is envisaged that monthly contributions to the NPS be roughly doubled in real terms by 2015, implying a rise of about 50 percent in contributions relative to household income.

The combined effect of these measures would be to raise social security contributions to 14½ percent of GDP by 2020 from the 9½ percent share in the absence of reform (Chart 5-3). As regards benefits, pension payments would be reduced to 20 percent of GDP by 2020 from the "unchanged parameters" level of 22½ percent. Together, these reforms would be sufficient to balance the EPIS and NPS components of the social security program. They would not, however, offset the rise in medical care costs, or the burden of rising government debt. This is evident in the middle panel of Chart 5-3, which shows that, although the overall deficit would narrow over the rest of this decade, it would start to widen beyond 2005. The subsequent rise in the deficit and the stock of debt in relation to GDP would be more gradual than in the absence of pension reform, but it is apparent that further measures would be needed to achieve a sustainable long-run fiscal position.

On the present-value basis described above, the remaining imbalance amounts to 2 percent of GDP. The

of the required actions can be obtained by comparing the discounted present values of government revenues and spending (in the absence of additional measures).[7] The resulting gap is a measure of the "fundamental"

---

[7] Specifically, the present value of primary expenditures plus the level of the initial debt stock is subtracted from the present value of revenues. Dividing the result by the present value of GDP indicates the actions that need to be taken—as a share of GDP, on a present-value basis—to stabilize the debt-to-GDP ratio over the long run and thus to achieve a sustainable fiscal position.

[8] For instance, if the required adjustments were postponed by five years until 2000, they would rise to 7¼ percent of GDP; if postponed until 2020, they would reach almost 11 percent of GDP.

[9] This long-term reform scenario has been constructed by the Ministry of Health and Welfare in conjunction with the latest five-year review of the pension system.

[10] The contribution rate would be raised in increments of roughly 2½ percentage points every five years, beginning in 1995–96.

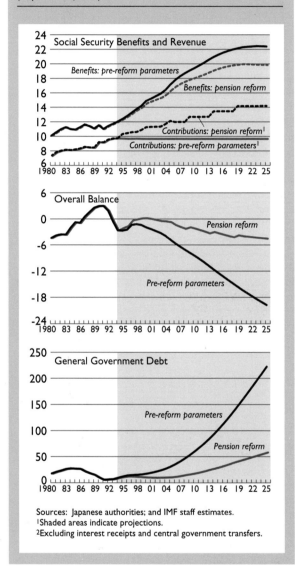

Chart 5-3. Long-Term Fiscal Projections: Pre-Reform Program Parameters Versus Pension Reform[1]

(In percent of GDP)

Sources: Japanese authorities; and IMF staff estimates.
[1]Shaded areas indicate projections.
[2]Excluding interest receipts and central government transfers.

ment.[11] An alternative approach on the revenue side could involve eliminating the special deduction for pension income in the personal income tax system.[12] Although it is difficult to assess the precise impact of such a reform in the absence of microeconomic tax data, a hypothetical rise in the average tax rate on public pension benefits of 30 percent would raise about 2 percent of GDP in additional revenues by 2000.

Implications for the Saving-Investment Balance

The long-term prospects for Japan's saving and investment depend on the behavior of public and private saving, as well as overall investment. Public saving will be determined by the policy actions taken to address population aging: as discussed above, pre-reform policies would lead to an explosive rise in the deficit and debt, whereas pension reform moderates the size and timing of the fiscal deterioration. Private saving will be influenced by the shift in the demographic structure itself, asset accumulation, and expectations of future social security benefits and tax liabilities. Finally, investment will depend on the desired capital-to-output ratio, the trend growth rate of output, and the depreciation rate of the capital stock.

Operationally, the projection for (gross) public saving is obtained as the sum of the overall government balance plus the rate of (gross) public investment, based on the fiscal scenarios described above. Private saving is determined residually as the difference between income and consumption: the latter moves in line with wealth, which is defined as the discounted value of labor income and social security benefits, less the discounted value of taxes and social security contributions, plus the stock of financial and physical wealth. In addition, consumption increases as the overall dependency ratio rises, with a response parameter given by the relationship between Japanese demographics and household behavior.[13] The desired capital-to-output ratio continues to grow in line with the declining relative price of capital goods. Gross investment is then determined by the investment needed to keep the capital stock growing in line with potential output and the desired capital-to-output rate, and by the depreciation rate (which is assumed to remain at its historical level).

required adjustment could be achieved in the form of either revenue or expenditure measures. Assuming that revenues are the source of adjustment, one solution would be to alter the consumption tax rate over the longer run to compensate for the rising social costs of an aging population. Beyond the rise in the consumption tax rate in 1997 that is incorporated in the baseline scenario, a further increase to roughly 10 percent would be needed by the end of the decade to achieve the required adjust-

---

[11] This is based on the authorities' estimate that each percentage point rise in the consumption tax generates about 0.4 percent of GDP in additional revenues. An option that would moderate the required rise in the tax rate would be to bring small businesses, which are currently tax-exempt, into the consumption tax base.

[12] In 1990, the tax-exempt threshold of a childless retired couple whose household head was aged 65 or over ranged from ¥3.1 trillion to ¥4.5 trillion, whereas for a working-age couple the threshold ranged from ¥1.7 trillion to ¥2.3 trillion (see Takayama (1992)).

[13] See Section IV of this volume for a discussion of the methodology.

Chart 5-4. Projected Long-Run Saving-Investment Balances: Pre-Reform Program Parameters Versus Pension Reform[1]

(In percent of GDP)

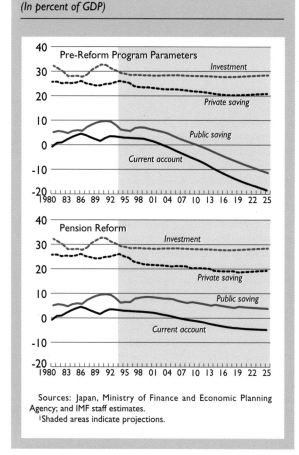

Sources: Japan, Ministry of Finance and Economic Planning Agency; and IMF staff estimates.

[1]Shaded areas indicate projections.

The projections for the components of saving and investment along with the implied current account balance are shown in Chart 5-4. Under the assumption of pre-reform social security parameters—and no other fiscal initiatives to deal with population aging—the dramatic rise in public dissaving is reinforced by a downward trend in the private saving rate. The investment ratio declines moderately until 2015, reflecting slowing growth in potential output, before rising slightly near the end of

the projection horizon. The net result is a swing in the external balance from a surplus of slightly over 2 percent of GDP in 2000 to a deficit of 15 percent of GDP by 2020. Such a huge deterioration in the external balance would almost certainly not be "financeable" in reality;[14] neither would the government deficits associated with an exploding debt stock find a ready market. Finally, predicting the response of private saving in the face of unsustainable fiscal policies is problematic when the eventual resolution of the situation is not specified. But the very unsustainability of these outcomes serves to underscore the imbalances that would potentially result from shifts in the Japanese demographic structure.

As shown in the lower panel of Chart 5-4, full implementation of the pension reform proposals sharply reduces the decline in public saving, which falls from 8½ to 4½ percent of GDP from 2000 to 2020. Nevertheless, combined with a 3 percentage point drop in the private saving rate over this period and roughly flat investment, the current account balance falls steadily to a deficit of about 5 percent of GDP by 2020. Although the decline is smaller than in the previous scenario, the underlying fiscal position would remain unsustainable, and further adjustments would be required to prevent both government debt and external liabilities from rising without bound beyond this horizon. Scenarios that incorporate the needed fiscal adjustments suggest that the current account deficit would stabilize in a range of 1–2 percent of GDP beyond 2015.

References

Feldman, Robert A., "Japan: Outlook for Social Expenditure, 1980–2025" (unpublished; Washington: International Monetary Fund, July 1985).

Takayama, Noriyuki, *The Greying of Japan: An Economic Perspective on Public Pensions*, Economic Research Series, No. 30 (Tokyo: Institute of Economic Research, Hitotsubashi University, 1992).

Van den Noord, Paul, and Richard Herd, "Pension Liabilities in the Seven Major Economies," Economics Department Working Paper 142 (Paris: Organization for Economic Cooperation and Development, 1993).

[14] Especially because several other large countries face problems associated with future population aging.

VI   Movements in Asset Prices Since the Mid-1980s

Juha Kähkönen

In the second half of the 1980s, Japan's stock prices tripled, and land prices doubled. The surge in asset prices was followed by a collapse in stock prices starting in early 1990 and by a more gradual downturn in land prices from mid-1990 onward. This section analyzes the causes of the asset price fluctuations and the effects of the fluctuations on economic growth.

The sharp movements in Japanese asset prices since the mid-1980s have led many observers to conclude that there was a speculative "bubble"—a continuous market overvaluation followed by a collapse. The evidence discussed below suggests that, in addition to this, "fundamentals" also played a significant role. In part, the increase in the prices of real estate and equities reflected the growth in the economy: in the second half of the 1980s, real GDP increased by 25 percent, and corporate profits rose by 69 percent. Another part of the asset price inflation is attributable to easy monetary policy, which led to a decline in interest rates—ten-year bond yields fell from 6.3 percent in 1985 to 4.2 percent in 1987—and to a consequent ballooning of the present values of future profits and rents. A third (but difficult to quantify) contributing factor was excessive risk taking associated with changes in the financial environment. Distortions in Japan's land tax system also accelerated the rise in asset prices. As regards the decline in asset prices since 1990, monetary tightening and measures designed to dampen the real estate market played key roles.

The swings in asset prices had a significant direct impact on economic growth, through wealth effects on consumption and through capital costs on investment. Estimates indicate that asset price increases boosted consumption by a cumulative 2–4 percent in the second half of the 1980s, whereas the impact on business fixed investment may have been as large as 10 percent. The downturn in asset prices since 1990 (which seems to have brought asset prices close to their trend levels) is estimated to have depressed real spending by roughly the same amounts in 1990–93. Besides the direct effects, asset prices have had indirect effects on the economy through money demand, bank profitability, and the financial system.

Developments Since the Mid-1980s

The dramatic rise in stock and land prices in the second half of the 1980s (Chart 6-1 and Table 6-1) was followed by a sharp decline in stock prices starting in early 1990 and a more moderate downturn in land prices from mid-1990 on. Although both stock and land prices had exhibited broad swings twice earlier in the postwar era (in the late 1950s and early 1970s), the strength of the recent asset price boom and the sharpness of the decline were unprecedented.

The Nikkei 225 stock price index rose at an annual average rate of 31 percent between end-1985 and end-1989 (Chart 6-2). During most of that period, the price-earnings ratio, which had averaged 21 during the first half of the decade, remained above 40. The first phase of the stock price boom saw the Nikkei 225 double from about 13,000 in December 1985 to the 26,000 range in October 1987. In the latter month, "Black Monday" reversed some of the increase, but, although the pace in most other stock markets leveled off, the Japanese stock market recovered quickly, and stock prices started climbing with fresh momentum. An all-time high in daily trading volume was recorded in July 1988, and the price index peaked on the last trading day of 1989, with the Nikkei 225 standing at almost 39,000. At that time, the market capitalization of the Tokyo Stock Exchange was $4.1 trillion (about 1.5 times Japan's GDP), compared with $0.9 trillion (equivalent to 60 percent of GDP) at the end of 1985. The size of the Japanese equity market had already surpassed that of the United States in 1987, and at the end of 1989 the Tokyo Stock Exchange accounted for 41 percent of total world equities.[1]

Land prices in Japan increased at an annual average rate of 13 percent between end-1985 and end-1990 (Chart 6-3). Compared with previous episodes of rapid land price increases, this boom had special features. First, it was unusually long, especially in comparison with the one in 1972–73. Second, in sharp contrast to the fairly uniform rises in land prices during earlier booms, there were large differences in land price increases with respect to location and land use. Although the price of land in

---

[1] Note, however, that in Japan cross-ownership of equity shares is more common than in other major countries. French and Poterba (1991) estimated that in the second half of the 1980s intercorporate equity holdings accounted for about half of the total market value of Japanese stocks, compared with 2 percent in the United States. Excluding cross-holdings, the market capitalization of Japanese stocks was about two thirds of that in the United States, and about 25 percent of the world total, at the end of 1989.

Chart 6-1. Movements in Asset Prices

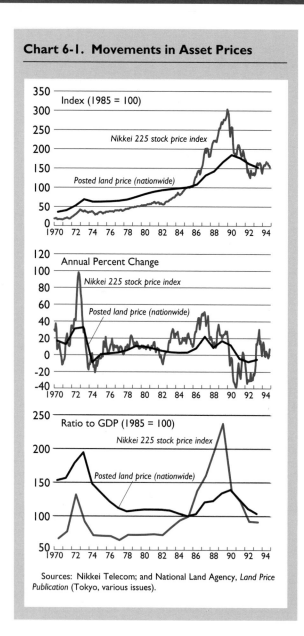

Sources: Nikkei Telecom; and National Land Agency, *Land Price Publication* (Tokyo, various issues).

Chart 6-2. Stock Price Developments

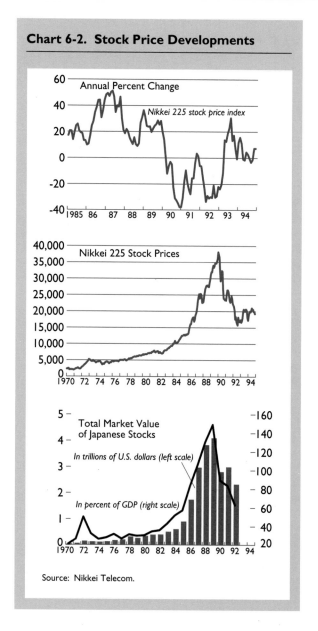

Source: Nikkei Telecom.

Tokyo doubled in 1986–87 alone, land prices outside the major cities rose by only 38 percent over the entire five-year period. The surge in land prices started in the mixed commercial-residential districts of central Tokyo and rapidly spread to Tokyo's residential areas. In 1988, when land prices in Tokyo started to stabilize, prices in Osaka and Nagoya, the other large metropolitan areas, accelerated. Land prices in the three metropolitan areas peaked at end-1990, when they were, on average, twice as high as in 1985. In all areas, commercial land increased in value faster than residential land, and the appreciation of industrial land lagged well behind both.

The downturn in asset prices began in 1990. A collapse of the Nikkei 225 index by 3 percent on February 21,

1990 started a sharp declining trend in stock prices. By year's end, the index had fallen by almost 40 percent from the peak, and the price-earnings ratio had declined to a level roughly in line with its trend level before the boom. The bottom in the stock price cycle was reached in August 1992, with the Nikkei 225 dipping briefly to about 14,000 (36 percent of the peak at the end of 1989). The Government's announcement in August 1992 of an economic stimulus package, however, helped the stock market to recover, and the Nikkei 225 subsequently stabilized in the 16,000–18,000 range. In late March 1993, expectations of another stimulus package led to a sharp increase in stock prices. Following the announcement of the second package in April, the increase in stock prices

Table 6-1. Asset Price Developments
(At end of year)

	1985	1986	1987	1988	1989	1990	1991	1992	1993
					Index, 1985 = 100				
Stock prices									
Nikkei 225	100.0	144.1	174.8	229.0	293.8	182.9	171.9	134.0	138.6
Land prices									
Nationwide	100.0	107.7	131.1	141.9	165.5	184.2	175.7	161.0	152.0
Commercial	100.0	113.4	138.2	152.5	177.9	200.9	192.9	170.9	151.6
Residential	100.0	107.6	134.5	145.1	169.8	188.0	177.4	162.0	154.4
Tokyo	100.0	123.8	204.6	208.3	223.3	239.0	218.9	186.3	168.8
Commercial	100.0	148.2	238.8	245.9	257.7	268.3	249.8	202.3	165.3
Residential	100.0	121.5	204.8	205.7	219.2	233.7	212.4	181.4	167.3
					In percent change				
Stock prices									
Nikkei 225	13.2	44.1	21.3	31.0	28.3	−37.7	−6.1	−22.0	3.4
Land prices									
Nationwide	2.6	7.7	21.7	8.3	16.6	11.3	−4.6	−8.4	−5.6
Commercial	5.1	13.4	21.9	10.3	16.7	12.9	−4.0	−11.4	−11.3
Residential	2.2	7.6	25.0	7.9	17.0	10.7	−5.6	−8.7	−4.7
Tokyo	4.1	23.8	65.3	1.8	7.2	7.0	−8.4	−14.9	−9.4
Commercial	12.5	48.2	61.1	3.0	4.8	4.1	−6.9	−19.0	−18.3
Residential	3.0	21.5	68.6	0.4	6.6	6.6	−9.1	−14.6	−7.8
					Ratio to GDP, 1985 = 100				
Stock prices									
Nikkei 225	100.0	138.0	160.7	197.6	237.6	138.1	122.2	92.4	94.6
Land prices									
Nationwide	100.0	103.1	120.5	122.5	133.9	139.0	124.9	110.9	103.7
Commercial	100.0	108.6	127.1	131.5	143.9	151.6	137.1	117.8	103.5
Residential	100.0	103.0	123.7	125.2	137.3	141.9	126.1	111.6	105.3
Tokyo	100.0	118.5	188.2	179.7	180.6	180.4	155.6	128.4	115.2
Commercial	100.0	141.9	219.6	212.1	208.4	202.5	177.5	139.4	112.8
Residential	100.0	116.3	188.4	177.4	177.3	176.4	151.0	125.0	114.1

Sources: Nikkei Telecom; and Japan, National Land Agency, *Land Price Publication* (Tokyo, various issues).

continued, and the Nikkei 225 reached 21,000 points—a level first recorded in March 1987—in mid-May 1993. With the yen appreciating and the recession continuing, the stock price index declined during the remainder of 1993, falling to about 16,000 in November 1993 amid signs of a further deterioration in the economic outlook. In the first half of 1994, the Nikkei climbed to a range of 20,000–21,000, reflecting both the adoption of further economic stimulus measures and signs of a bottoming out of the recession.

The rise in land prices came to a halt in mid-1990. At the same time, the number of land transactions, which had risen dramatically during the boom, fell signifi-

cantly.[2] Land prices in large cities started to fall toward the end of 1990—modestly at first, but later at an increasing pace. At the end of 1992, land prices in the three metropolitan areas were 25 percent below their level at the end of 1990, and further declines were recorded in 1993 before prices started to stabilize in 1994. By contrast, the price of land outside the large cities has been

_____

[2] If the tax revenue from real estate acquisition (adjusted for the increase in the assessment value of the tax base) is taken as an indicator, land transactions fell by 11 percent in 1990 and by 6 percent in 1991.

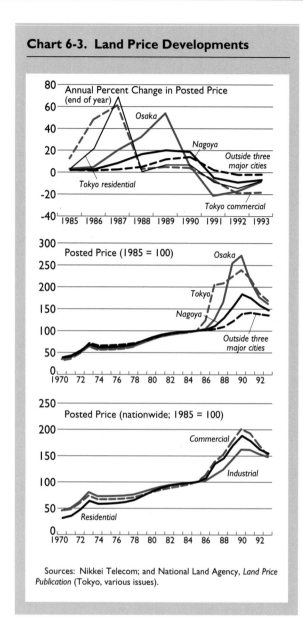

Chart 6-3. Land Price Developments

Annual Percent Change in Posted Price (end of year)

Osaka

Nagoya

Outside three major cities

Tokyo residential

Tokyo commercial

Posted Price (1985 = 100)

Osaka

Tokyo

Nagoya

Outside three major cities

Posted Price (nationwide; 1985 = 100)

Commercial

Industrial

Residential

Sources: Nikkei Telecom; and National Land Agency, *Land Price Publication* (Tokyo, various issues).

relatively stable since 1990, and the decline in the price of land for industrial use has been small.

Causes of Asset Price Inflation and Deflation

Role of Fundamentals

Theoretically, the price of an asset (P) should equal the discounted present value of the expected earnings (E) on that asset. The discount factor is the rate of return on a risk-free asset (r) adjusted for the expected growth in earnings (g), taxes (t), and a risk premium (σ):

$$P = E/(r - g + t + \sigma). \qquad (6\text{-}1)$$

Thus, an increase in the price-earnings ratio of an asset could reflect one or more of the following factors: lower interest rates, improved prospects for earnings, lower taxation of the asset, and a reduced risk premium. Although arbitrage usually keeps actual asset prices at or near theoretical values determined by the fundamentals, there can be periods of speculative bubbles when market participants rationalize their purchases with the view that assets can be sold to someone else at an even higher price.

Much of the Japanese asset price inflation and deflation since 1985 can be explained by movements in the fundamentals (Chart 6-4). These movements reflect both policy actions and exogenous influences. First, interest rates have fluctuated widely, suggesting that monetary policy influenced movements in asset prices. In the second half of the 1980s, interest rates declined to historically low levels, reflecting a substantial easing of monetary policy. To counter the deflationary impact of the sharp appreciation of the yen after the Plaza accord in September 1985, the official discount rate was halved from 5 percent to 2.5 percent—the lowest rate ever—between January 1986 and February 1987. Long-term interest rates also fell, albeit not as sharply. Although the Japanese economy started a strong recovery in 1987, the easy stance of monetary policy was maintained, as events following Black Monday in October 1987 (a worldwide collapse in the stock markets and a sharp depreciation of the U.S. dollar) led to a coordinated easing of monetary conditions in all major industrial countries. In addition, the authorities felt external pressure to reduce the current account surplus by expanding domestic demand.

In the event, the official discount rate was not raised until May 1989; by August 1990, however, the rate had been increased several times to reach 6 percent. Long-term interest rates did not respond immediately, but by early 1990 they were back to levels before the boom. Many observers suggest that market expectations of a sharp rise in interest rates were the proximate cause for the February 21, 1990 collapse of the Tokyo Stock Exchange that marked the beginning of the sharp downturn in stock prices. Prompted by signs of a recession in the Japanese economy, the official discount rate was lowered several times between July 1991 and September 1993, and at the end of 1994 it stood at 1.75 percent, with long-term rates at historically low levels.

Second, expectations of growth in earnings from assets are likely to have changed since the mid-1980s. After being almost stagnant in the first half of the 1980s, corporate profits increased by 69 percent in the second half of the decade, and this buoyancy could have created expectations of permanently higher growth opportunities and may have contributed to higher stock prices. Although rents increased no faster than nominal GDP, expectations of large capital gains are likely to have fueled land price increases. The second half of the 1980s also witnessed deregulation and structural changes in the Japanese economy (the latter in part reflecting the need for firms to adjust to a permanently stronger yen), which

Chart 6-4. Asset Prices and "Fundamentals"

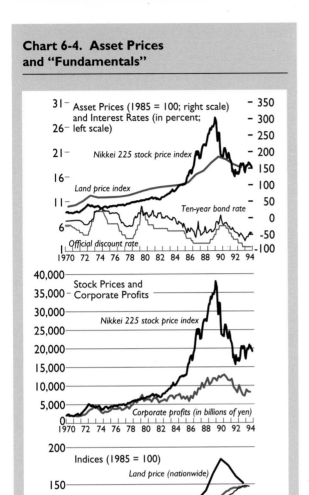

Sources: Japan, Economic Planning Agency (EPA), *Annual Report on National Accounts* (Tokyo, 1993); and Bank of Japan, *Short-Term Survey of Business Enterprises* and *Economic Statistics Monthly* (Tokyo, various issues).

tionary features are low assessment of property and inheritance taxes (thus reducing the cost of holding land relative to other assets and making land the preferred asset for inheritance); high rates of capital gains tax (thus discouraging land sales); and lighter taxation of agricultural land (thus raising the price of nonagricultural land).[4]

Although distortionary land taxation can explain the high *level* of land prices in Japan, changes in the tax system are needed to explain land price *movements*. Since the mid-1980s, there indeed were such changes. One of them—an observed fall in the property tax assessment ratio—contributed to the surge in land prices.[5] Most of them, however, represented attempts to curb land price increases. In 1987, the Government introduced a heavy surcharge on capital gains from short-term trading, with a view to reducing speculative transactions, and reduced the long-term holding period (subject to a lower rate) to promote the supply of land. In 1990, the Tax Advisory Commission submitted to the Prime Minister a report entitled "Basic Recommendations on the Ideal Framework of Land Taxation" (Japan (1990)), and some of the recommendations were included in the 1991 Land Tax Bill.[6] The new Bill, which came into effect in fiscal years 1991 and 1992, was intended to improve efficiency and equity in land use by encouraging the transfer of land to residential uses and by putting downward pressure on real estate prices. A key change in the Bill was the introduction of a land value tax (a tax on land holdings), initially at a rate of 0.2 percent and since 1993 at a rate of 0.3 percent. Other changes included phased increases in the assessment ratios of property and inheritance taxes, a higher long-term capital gains tax, and removal of many special treatments of agricultural land.

Finally, some researchers have claimed that the risk premium on Japanese equities declined in the second half of the 1980s. In particular, Ueda (1990) estimated the premium to have fallen to about ½ of 1 percent in 1986–88 from an average of 5 percent during the preceding ten years. Possible reasons for the decline in the risk premium include a change in the distribution of wealth toward less risk-averse investors (such as large institutional investors) and an increase in the wealth of the average investor (which would tend to reduce the degree of relative risk aversion).

may have created widespread optimism about the growth prospects of the economy.

Third, taxation had an impact on land prices. In Japan, land has traditionally been taxed more lightly than other assets, and this has contributed to Japanese land prices being among the highest in the world.[3] The key distor-

---

[3] See Ishi (1991) and Takagi (1989) for descriptions of land taxation in Japan, and Sachs and Boone (1988) and Ito (1992, pp. 408–14) for international comparisons.

[4] An econometric study by Ando and others (1989) concluded that taxing farmland at the same rate as land for housing would be a highly effective means of raising the supply of land for residential uses and lowering land prices.

[5] Ishi (1991) estimated that, whereas in the early 1980s property tax assessment was on average two thirds of the official valuation (which in turn is estimated to be only 70–80 percent of the market price), by 1988 the ratio had declined to about one half and by 1991 to slightly over one third.

[6] For details of the land tax reform, see Organization for Economic Cooperation and Development (1991, pp. 153–54).

Changes in the Financial Environment

There is widespread agreement that, in addition to the standard fundamentals discussed above, changes in the financial environment in the 1980s contributed significantly to the sharp rise in asset prices.[7] These changes were brought about by extensive financial liberalization and innovation, and they were evident in increased lending to real estate and in vigorous financial investment activities of households and nonfinancial corporations.

Japan had entered the 1980s with a tightly regulated financial system, but during the decade extensive reforms were instituted: controls on capital movements were dismantled; interest rates on deposits were deregulated; and markets were introduced for a number of new instruments (such as commercial paper, futures, and options). The deregulation went a long way toward enhancing competition and improving the efficiency of the financial system, but it also gave rise to two major developments that fueled asset price inflation in the late 1980s. First, bank and nonbank lending to the real estate sector increased sharply because of changes in the behavior of both lenders and borrowers. As large manufacturing corporations gained access to international capital markets and to an increasingly developed domestic securities market, their reliance on bank loans declined dramatically, making small and medium-sized enterprises and households primary customers of banks and releasing loanable funds to nonmanufacturing sectors, especially real estate. This shift led to an apparent increase in the riskiness of banks' loan portfolios, but increased competition prevented lending rates from rising sufficiently to compensate for the higher risk. By end-1989, bank loans outstanding to real-estate-related activities had more than doubled in value since 1985 and accounted for almost one fourth of the banks' total loan portfolio.[8] During this period, nonbanks, which are more lightly regulated than banks, were even more aggressive than banks in financing real estate transactions. Second, the liberalized financial environment, together with the easy monetary conditions prevailing in the second half of the 1980s, gave nonfinancial corporations opportunities for financial arbitrage and improved credit availability for households. As a result, financial investment increased sharply and was to a significant extent channeled into the stock market, driving up equity prices.

Besides directly influencing asset prices, the financial markets also helped the increases in land and equity prices to reinforce each other. Higher land prices can be perceived by investors as an increase in the market value of firms, and this raises stock prices. Higher land prices also increase the value of land as a collateral, enabling

landowners to obtain more bank loans. Some of the additional loans can be used for further land and equity purchases, which will further raise asset prices. Although this description does not establish the ultimate cause for the asset price increases, it is suggestive of a multiplier process that works through the financial markets once one asset price starts to increase.

Throughout most of the bubble period, the Japanese authorities chose not to intervene in the financial markets. However, as part of a series of special measures to contain land prices (reforms in land taxation constituted the main part), the Government in April 1990 placed quantitative restrictions on bank lending to the real estate sector. Once the declining trend in land prices became apparent, these restrictions were lifted at the end of 1991. In May 1991, the Government also amended the legislation regulating the lending industry, with a view to strengthening restraints on nonbank lending for land-related purposes.

Was There a Bubble?

Practically all empirical studies attempting to explain Japanese asset price movements since the mid-1980s have concluded that there was a speculative bubble; that is, fundamentals alone are unable to explain the sharp increases in the second half of the 1980s and the subsequent collapse.[9] These studies typically have estimated an equation such as equation (6-1) using data from the period before the bubble and have compared predictions for the postsample with actual developments. To shed light on the relative importance of various fundamentals and the possible existence of a bubble, the next few paragraphs describe the results of two simple exercises.

First, an error-correction equation was estimated for stock prices using quarterly data from 1981 to 1985, with corporate profits and long-term interest rates as dependent variables (data on risk premiums and taxes on equity holdings were not readily available):

$$\Delta \log (PEQ/PROFT)$$
$$= 0.22 - 0.03 \; \Delta(RLB - PROFT\%)$$
$$ (3.4) \quad (2.4)$$
$$ - 0.06 \; (RLB - PROFT\%)_{-1}$$
$$ (3.3)$$
$$ + 0.49 \; \Delta \log (PEQ/PROFT)_{-1}$$
$$ (2.3)$$
$$ - 0.36 \; \log (PEQ/PROFT)_{-1}$$
$$ (3.1) \qquad\qquad (6\text{-}2)$$

$$R^2 = 0.49 \qquad DW = 1.88 \qquad h = 0.44,$$

---

[7] See Japan (1993) for a detailed discussion of the impact of the changed financial environment on asset price inflation.

[8] This estimate includes bank loans to nonbanks for real-estate-related purposes.

[9] As regards stock prices, representative studies include Bank of Japan (1993), French and Poterba (1991), Hardouvelis (1988), Hoshi and Kashyap (1990), Ogawa (1993), and Ueda (1990). For land prices, recent studies include Japan (1992), Japan (1993), and the Japan Economic Research Center (1993).

where

PEQ	=	Nikkei 225 stock price index
PROFT	=	trend of corporate profits
PROFT%	=	trend growth in corporate profits
RLB	=	ten-year government bond rate
R^2	=	coefficient of determination
DW	=	Durbin-Watson statistic
h	=	Durbin's *h* statistic

and the numbers in parentheses are *t*-statistics. Note that this equation implies a long-run elasticity of stock prices with respect to the interest rate of $-\frac{1}{6}$. Thus, a 1 percentage point drop in the long-run interest rate should lead to a permanent 17 percent increase in stock prices.

Equation (6-2), which explains stock price movements in the period before the bubble reasonably well, was then used to predict developments from 1986 on (Chart 6-5). Several conclusions emerge. First, if interest rates had remained at their 1985 levels and expected profits had grown at the historical trend rate, stock prices would have risen at an annual rate of 6 percent—far below the actual rate observed during the bubble period. Second, the simulations imply that monetary policy contributed more to the collapse in stock prices than it did to the long rise of those prices: although the contribution of lower interest rates to the boom in stock prices in 1986–89 is estimated at 15 percent, higher interest rates accounted for as much as 45 percent of the sharp decline in equity prices in 1990.[10] Furthermore, lower interest rates since mid-1991 helped to keep stock prices from falling even more rapidly than they actually did. Third, albeit difficult to measure, changed expectations about corporate profit growth could potentially explain a major part of the boom and the collapse in stock prices. The black line in the middle panel of Chart 6-5 indicates how much the expected growth rate of corporate profits would have had to differ from the historical trend in order to fully explain actual movements in stock prices. As can be seen from the chart, the rise in stock prices in 1986–89 would have been consistent with an increase in the expected profit growth rate from 6 percent to almost 10 percent—not an unreasonably large change, given the underlying growth rate of actual profits at the time and the increase in the share of profits in GDP. Part of the increase in corporate profits was cyclical, however, and should not have affected a rational investor's valuation of equity. Hence, the possibility of a bubble cannot be excluded.

A similar exercise was carried out for land prices. With potential GDP growth used as a proxy for the

---

[10] Nevertheless, below-trend interest rates (easy monetary policy) had a significant direct impact on the rise in stock prices in 1986–89: the equation suggests that in the peak year 1989 stock prices were 20 percent higher than they would have been had interest rates remained at levels recorded before the bubble.

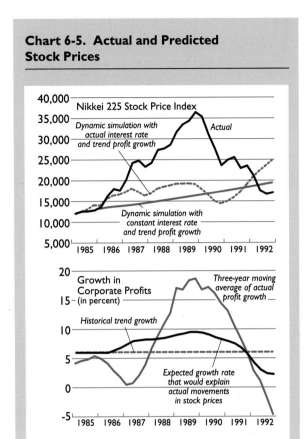

Chart 6-5. Actual and Predicted Stock Prices

Sources: Nikkei Telecom; and IMF staff estimates.

expected increase in real rents, the estimated equation took the following form (the data were from the period 1970–85):

$$\Delta \log (PLAND/YT) =$$
$$-\ 0.40 - 0.0044(RLB - PEXP - QT\%)$$
$$\quad (2.2) \quad (1.7)$$
$$+\ 0.61\ \Delta \log (PLAND/YT)_{-1}$$
$$\quad (5.7)$$
$$-\ 0.051\ \log (PLAND/YT)_{-1}$$
$$\quad (2.2) \hspace{6cm} (6\text{-}3)$$
$$R^2 = 0.41 \qquad DW = 1.90 \qquad h = -0.89,$$

where

PLAND = nationwide land price index
YT   = growth rate of nominal potential GDP
RLB   = ten-year government bond rate
PEXP = expected inflation rate
QT%   = growth rate of potential GDP.

Equation (6-3) implies a long-run interest rate elasticity of land prices of −0.12, similar to that estimated for stock prices.

Dynamic simulations over the period 1986–92 suggest the following conclusions (Chart 6-6). First, as in the case of stock prices, easy monetary policy (low interest rates) explains about 15 percent of the increase in land prices (over and above the estimated trend increase of 8½ percent) during 1986–89. Tighter monetary policy in 1989–90 helped to bring land prices down, but the fall in land prices continued unabated in 1991–92 despite an easing of monetary conditions. Second, the simulations do not suggest a significant role for changed expectations about rent growth, leaving the bulk of the land price increase in the second half of the 1980s unexplained (see Chart 6-6). Although this could simply reflect a low correlation of potential GDP growth with the difficult-to-measure expectations about growth in earnings from land, it could not signal the existence of a bubble.

Note that the two simple exercises undertaken above both suggest that equity and land prices may have returned close to their trend levels in 1992: in Charts 6-5 and 6-6, the lines indicating the underlying trend growth based on experience before the bubble cross the lines representing actual developments. There are, however, factors not included in the estimated models that may

suggest otherwise. In particular, the changes in land taxation contained in the 1991 Land Tax Bill may have made the decline in land prices deeper and longer-lasting than equation (6-3) would imply. This could explain why land prices have continued to fall while stock prices have started to recover.

Impact of Asset Price Movements on the Economy

Even though the reasons for the sharp fluctuations of asset prices may not be completely understood, there is little doubt that these fluctuations contributed to the long boom in the Japanese economy that began in 1986 and to the recession that started in 1991. This part of the section discusses the effects of asset prices on economic growth, mainly through private consumption and investment, which contributed 2½ percentage points and 2¾ percentage points, respectively, to the average GDP growth of 5 percent in 1987–90.

The wide fluctuations in asset prices had a direct impact on *consumption* expenditure through the wealth effect. Household net worth increased sharply in the second half of the 1980s, from the equivalent of 5½ times annual household disposable income at end-1985 to almost 8¾ times such income by end-1989 (Chart 6-7 and Table 6-2). Capital gains on land holdings (which account for about half of total household assets) were responsible for 70 percent of the rise in net wealth over this period, with stock holdings (less than 10 percent of the total) accounting for another 13 percent. Following a turn-around in asset prices, the household net worth position deteriorated in 1990 as a ratio of disposable income and, in 1991, also in absolute terms. Although comprehensive data are not available, net worth is estimated to have fallen further by some 5 percent in 1992, with the ratio of net worth to household income estimated to have dipped to below the 1987 level.

Compared with the sharp swings in asset prices, the direct effect on consumption appears to be relatively small. Estimates of the positive effect during the upswing typically range between ⅓ of 1 percentage point and 1 percentage point a year; on the same basis, the decline in asset prices in 1991–92 is estimated to have resulted in an annual decline in consumption of ¼ to ¾ of 1 percentage point.[11] The low estimates are obtained by applying typical estimates of the propensity to consume out of wealth (ranging from 0.03 in MULTIMOD, the IMF's multicountry macroeconometric model, to 0.06 in Japan (1992)) to changes in real *financial wealth* (which accounts for slightly over one third of total household wealth in Japan). The high estimates are based on move-

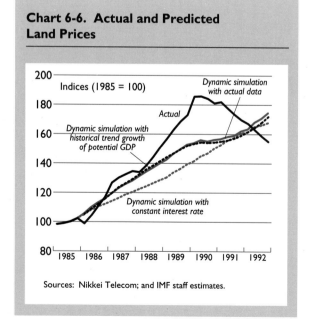

Chart 6-6. Actual and Predicted Land Prices

Indices (1985 = 100)

Dynamic simulation with actual data

Actual

Dynamic simulation with historical trend growth of potential GDP

Dynamic simulation with constant interest rate

Sources: Nikkei Telecom; and IMF staff estimates.

----

[11] Real private consumption grew at an average annual rate of 5½ percent during 1987–90 and 4¼ percent during 1991–92.

Table 6-2. Consolidated Balance Sheet of Household Sector

	1985	1986	1987	1988	1989	1990	1991	1992
	In trillions of yen							
Total assets	1,433.0	1,671.7	2,024.6	2,235.7	2,591.5	2,718.1	2,665.3	2,520.5
Inventories	9.1	8.6	8.8	8.8	9.2	9.6	9.8	9.4
Net fixed assets	171.1	173.2	184.0	194.0	212.3	227.4	238.6	244.5
Nonreproducible tangible assets	693.5	857.4	1,116.7	1,216.6	1,411.3	1,531.5	1,413.1	1,273.0
Land	664.7	827.1	1,085.9	1,183.2	1,376.7	1,495.0	1,374.4	1,233.8
Financial assets	559.3	632.5	715.1	816.3	958.7	949.6	1,003.8	993.7
Currency	20.3	22.7	24.8	27.4	31.9	32.2	33.0	33.2
Transferable deposits	33.7	37.0	41.3	44.8	52.9	53.6	56.0	58.5
Other deposits	296.4	314.6	337.4	362.3	397.6	438.7	477.9	504.6
Long-term bonds	50.9	53.5	60.4	59.7	66.2	69.1	65.9	64.2
Corporate shares	65.9	96.1	123.7	173.4	237.3	162.7	161.8	107.3
Net equity in life insurance and pensions	80.6	95.1	112.3	133.2	155.5	173.6	189.4	205.5
Other financial assets	11.5	13.5	15.2	15.5	17.3	19.7	19.8	20.5
Total liabilities	195.8	211.0	238.7	265.5	294.1	325.1	341.1	340.5
Loans by private sector	113.2	128.0	150.5	167.8	194.5	214.6	222.7	224.6
Loans by public sector	37.7	40.0	43.3	45.9	50.3	53.5	57.6	61.1
Trade credit	44.9	43.0	44.9	51.8	49.4	56.9	60.8	54.8
Net worth	1,237.2	1,460.7	1,785.9	1,970.2	2,297.4	2,393.0	2,342.2	2,180.0
	In annual percent change							
Total assets	7.4	16.7	21.1	10.4	15.9	4.9	−1.9	−5.4
Land	7.5	24.4	31.3	9.0	16.4	8.6	−8.1	−10.2
Financial assets	9.3	13.1	13.1	14.2	17.4	−0.9	5.7	−1.0
Corporate shares	16.4	45.8	28.7	40.2	36.9	−31.4	−0.6	−33.7
Total liabilities	6.8	7.8	13.1	11.2	10.8	10.5	4.9	0.2
Net worth	7.5	18.1	22.3	10.3	16.6	4.2	−2.9	−6.2
	Ratio to disposable income							
Total assets	6.5	7.3	8.6	9.0	9.8	9.7	9.0	8.3
Land	3.0	3.6	4.6	4.8	5.2	5.3	4.6	4.0
Financial assets	2.5	2.7	3.0	3.3	3.6	3.4	3.4	3.3
Corporate shares	0.3	0.4	0.5	0.7	0.9	0.6	0.5	0.4
Total liabilities	0.9	0.9	1.0	1.1	1.1	1.2	1.2	1.1
Net worth	5.6	6.3	7.5	8.0	8.7	8.5	7.8	7.2
Memorandum								
Real net worth								
In trillions of yen (1985 prices)	1,237.2	1,454.9	1,775.2	1,960.4	2,247.9	2,283.4	2,162.0	1,987.2
Percent change	5.1	17.6	22.0	10.4	14.7	1.6	−5.2	−8.1
Debt-to-asset ratio	13.7	12.6	11.8	11.9	11.3	12.0	12.8	13.5
Household disposable income								
In trillions of yen	220.7	230.3	236.7	247.7	263.9	280.0	296.1	304.8
Percent change	5.3	4.3	2.8	4.6	6.5	6.1	5.8	2.9
Ratio to disposable income (in percent)								
Gross interest payments	5.3	5.3	5.3	5.3	5.3	6.5	6.9	6.2
Consumer debt	0.5	0.6	0.6	0.6	0.7	0.9	1.1	1.0
Housing debt	2.1	2.1	2.1	2.2	2.3	2.9	3.1	2.9
Other	2.6	2.6	2.7	2.5	2.3	2.6	2.7	2.3
Net interest income	6.0	5.9	4.8	4.1	3.7	4.6	5.3	4.2

Source: Japan, Economic Planning Agency (EPA), *Annual Report on National Accounts* (Tokyo, 1993).
[1]IMF staff estimates based on land and stock price developments.

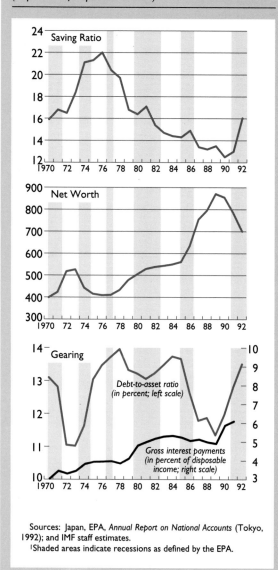

Chart 6-7. Household Saving and Net Wealth[1]

(In percent of disposable income)

Sources: Japan, EPA, *Annual Report on National Accounts* (Tokyo, 1992); and IMF staff estimates.

[1]Shaded areas indicate recessions as defined by the EPA.

increased consumption of homeowners was larger than the decreased consumption of renters. Thus, the high-end estimates mentioned above cannot be dismissed as implausible. Nevertheless, it is clear that changes in disposable income rather than swings in asset prices have accounted for the bulk of the growth in consumption since the mid-1980s.

The second half of the 1980s also saw a boom in *business fixed investment*, to which asset prices contributed by lowering capital costs and increasing the firms' net worth that could be used as collateral. Between 1986 and 1990, business fixed investment rose by 55 percent. Rapidly rising equity prices enabled large companies to shift from bank loans to issuing new stocks and equity-linked bonds at very low interest rates; buyers accepted the low rates because of the anticipation that the bonds could be converted into equities at favorable prices. Surging land prices in turn improved the capacity of small and medium-sized firms to raise bank loans with land as collateral.[12] For the nonfinancial corporate sector as a whole, leverage (debt-to-equity ratio) fell sharply, and liquidity rose along with capital spending, contrary to historical experience in Japan and the experience of many other industrial countries (Table 6-3).

With the decline in asset prices since 1990, there have been reverse effects on capital spending. Capital costs have risen. The collapse of stock prices has made it difficult for firms to raise new capital through equity issuance, and outstanding issues of equity-linked bonds are being redeemed. These developments have led large companies to return to bank loans and straight-bond issues, at a significantly higher cost than in the late 1980s. For small and medium-sized companies, the erosion of collateral land values has reduced borrowing opportunities, and the liquidity position of the entire nonfinancial business sector has declined to a level that prevailed in the early 1980s. The debt-equity ratio, which at the end of 1989 was only one third of its 1985 level, almost doubled in 1990–91 and is tentatively estimated to have returned to the pre-bubble level in 1992. The business sector's current financial difficulties and their impact on capital spending should not, however, be exaggerated. Although the financial position of firms has declined sharply over the past two to three years, this represents more a return to a normal situation following overheating than a plunge to historical lows.

In contrast to consumption, there are few representative estimates of the impact of asset price movements on business fixed investment, in part because of the difficulty of measuring capital costs and separating the effect of asset price changes from that of changes in monetary

ments in *total wealth*, including land. Most studies have argued (and found empirically) that land holdings have little or no effect on consumption in Japan: landowning households may not regard unrealized capital gains fully as changes in their real wealth, and consumers without land will have to increase their saving to obtain financing for costlier housing. An exception is a study by Dekle (1990), which used time-series and panel data for Japanese prefectures and concluded that the rise in land prices did have a positive effect on consumption, since the

---

[12] Ogawa (1993) has discussed recent literature that implies a positive relationship between the collateral value of the firm and the level of investment. His empirical work found evidence supporting this hypothesis.

Table 6-3. Consolidated Balance Sheet of Nonfinancial Incorporated Enterprises

	1985	1986	1987	1988	1989	1990	1991	1992
					In trillions of yen			
Total assets	1,095.5	1,238.8	1,470.0	1,666.7	1,912.3	1,983.3	1,969.8	1,830.6
Stocks	58.9	55.9	56.2	58.2	63.4	67.3	69.3	69.9
Net fixed assets	299.1	312.6	330.9	355.2	394.7	437.0	479.4	503.7
Nonreproducible tangible assets	261.7	327.7	442.6	497.3	592.4	674.2	617.1	553.6
Land	252.9	318.6	433.0	487.6	582.1	663.7	606.8	543.2
Financial assets	475.8	542.6	640.3	756.0	861.8	804.8	803.9	703.4
Currency	2.3	2.5	2.8	3.1	3.5	3.6	3.7	3.7
Transferable deposits	40.1	44.9	43.1	46.4	35.7	39.0	48.1	50.9
Other deposits	89.2	107.5	138.6	159.2	183.7	179.3	162.3	158.6
Short-term bills and bonds	0.4	1.2	0.3	0.2	—	0.4	—	0.8
Long-term bonds	11.7	12.7	13.0	12.1	11.6	12.5	13.3	12.0
Corporate shares	88.3	141.1	181.3	250.7	339.7	236.0	230.9	150.7
Net equity in life	—	—	0.1	1.8	2.8	5.1	4.2	3.9
insurance and pensions	—	—	—	—	—	—	—	—
Trade credit	204.0	194.1	222.4	239.7	231.6	253.4	268.4	249.2
Other financial assets	39.9	38.5	38.8	42.8	53.1	75.4	73.1	73.5
Total liabilities	758.5	891.2	1,022.7	1,234.6	1,497.2	1,350.8	1,394.6	1,248.3
Liabilities, excluding corporate shares	562.5	589.6	655.7	714.8	770.8	855.2	907.2	916.8
Short-term bills and bonds	1.6	1.7	1.5	0.9	0.7	0.5	0.4	0.2
Long-term bonds	56.2	62.2	68.6	74.3	85.8	98.5	111.2	114.3
Commercial paper	—	—	1.7	9.3	13.1	15.8	12.4	12.2
Loans by private sector	273.5	301.4	327.2	357.2	395.2	434.7	458.8	471.3
Loans by public sector	63.0	64.3	65.1	67.2	71.1	73.2	78.1	82.7
Trade credit	157.2	149.0	175.4	185.6	179.7	193.9	204.9	191.5
Other liabilities	11.0	10.9	16.2	20.3	25.2	38.5	41.5	44.6
Corporate shares	196.0	301.6	367.0	519.8	726.4	495.7	487.3	331.5
Net worth	337.0	347.6	447.3	432.1	415.1	632.5	575.2	582.3
					In annual percent change			
Total assets	7.9	13.1	18.7	13.4	14.7	3.7	−0.7	−7.1
Land	9.2	26.0	35.9	12.6	19.4	14.0	−8.6	−10.5
Financial assets	10.1	14.0	18.0	18.1	14.0	−6.6	−0.1	−12.5
Corporate shares	17.0	59.8	28.5	38.3	35.5	−30.5	−2.2	−34.7
Total liabilities	8.5	17.5	14.8	20.7	21.3	−9.8	3.2	−10.5
Liabilities, excluding corporate shares	6.4	4.8	11.2	9.0	7.8	10.9	6.1	1.1
Corporate shares	15.0	53.9	21.7	41.6	39.7	−31.8	−1.7	−32.0
Net worth	6.6	3.1	28.7	−3.4	−3.9	52.4	−9.1	1.2
Memorandum								
Operating surplus								
In trillions of yen	49.7	51.5	53.5	59.0	63.7	68.6	69.5	62.5
Percent change	9.3	3.6	3.7	10.4	8.0	7.6	1.4	—
Debt-to-equity ratio	2.0	1.4	1.3	1.0	0.8	1.3	1.4	2.1
Assets/profits	20.2	21.3	24.1	24.0	24.7	25.5	25.0	24.1
Land	5.1	6.2	8.1	8.3	9.1	9.7	8.7	7.8
Other assets	15.2	15.1	16.0	15.7	15.5	15.8	16.3	16.3
Liabilities/profits	11.3	11.4	12.3	12.1	12.1	12.5	13.0	13.2
Net worth/profits	8.9	9.9	11.8	11.9	12.6	13.0	12.0	11.0

Source: Japan, EPA, *Annual Report on National Accounts* (Tokyo, 1993).

conditions. MULTIMOD simulations suggest that a 1,000 point rise in the Nikkei 225 index would result in an increase of ½ of 1 percent to 1 percent in business fixed investment over two years. This implies that the surge in equity prices in 1986–89 raised investment cumulatively by almost 10 percent over 1987–90, accounting for one third of the acceleration in the growth of investment. On the same basis, the decline in equity prices in 1990–92, which brought the Nikkei 225 to below its level of the end of 1985, is estimated to have depressed investment by a cumulative 10 percent over 1991–93.

Residential investment increased by almost 50 percent during the early part of the boom before stabilizing in 1989. Although the boom in housing construction was driven by many of the same factors that caused the asset price inflation—low interest rates in particular—asset prices had an independent influence on residential investment through two channels. Besides the wealth effect, which tended to raise the demand for housing construction during the boom, higher land prices contained the demand for housing by households that did not own land and stimulated the supply of land for construction by owners of surplus land, making the impact of higher land prices on residential investment ambiguous. As in the case of business fixed investment, there are few empirical estimates. There is, however, some evidence that higher land prices had a differential impact on various types of residential investment: negative for owner-occupied housing, and positive for rental housing in Tokyo (Japan (1992, pp. 46–56)). All in all, the surge in asset prices does not appear to have been the driving force behind the boom in residential construction. Similarly, the collapse of land and equity prices is unlikely to have been the main contributing factor in the decline in residential construction in 1991–92.

References

Ando, Itaru, and others, "Econometric Analysis of Property Tax on Land," paper presented at the International Symposium on Structural Problems in the Japanese and World Economy, Economic Planning Agency, Tokyo, October 1989.

Bank of Japan, *Functions of Stock Markets: Implications for Corporate Financial Activities*, Special Paper 225 (Tokyo, February 1993).

Dekle, Robert, "Alternative Estimates of Japanese Saving and Comparisons with the U.S.: Can the Capital Gains to Land Be Included in Saving?" Institute for Economic Development Discussion Paper Series, No. 13 (Boston, Massachusetts: Boston University, December 1990).

French, Kenneth R., and James M. Poterba, "Were Japanese Stock Prices Too High?" *Journal of Financial Economics*, Vol. 29 (October 1991), pp. 337–63.

Hardouvelis, Gikas A., *Evidence on Stock Market Speculative Bubbles: Japan, United States, and Great Britain*, Federal Reserve Bank of New York Research Paper 8810 (New York, April 1988).

Hoshi, Takeo, and Anil K. Kashyap, "Evidence on *q* and Investment for Japanese Firms," *Journal of the Japanese and International Economies*, Vol. 4 (December 1990), pp. 371–400.

Ishi, Hiromitsu, "Land Tax Reform in Japan," *Hitotsubashi Journal of Economics*, Vol. 32 (June 1991), pp. 1–20.

Ito, Takatoshi, *The Japanese Economy* (Cambridge, Massachusetts: MIT Press, 1992).

Japan, Economic Planning Agency (EPA), *Economic Survey of Japan* (Tokyo, 1992 and various issues).

Japan, Economic Research Center, *Scenario to Renewed Growth: Japan's Economic Outlook, FY 1993–97* (Tokyo 1993).

Japan, Ministry of Finance, Institute of Fiscal and Monetary Policy, *The Mechanism and Economic Effects of Asset Price Fluctuations*, Report of the Research Committee (Tokyo, April 1993).

Japan, Tax Advisory Commission, "Basic Recommendations on the Ideal Framework of Land Taxation" (Tokyo, 1990).

Ogawa, Kazuo, "Asset Markets and Business Fluctuations in Japan," paper presented at the 10th International Symposium of the EPA, Business Cycle and Financial Policy Coordination, Tokyo, March 24–25, 1993.

Organization for Economic Cooperation and Development, *OECD Economic Surveys: Japan, 1990/91* (Paris, 1991).

Sachs, Jeffrey, and Peter Boone, "Japanese Structural Adjustment and the Balance of Payments," *Journal of the Japanese and International Economies*, Vol. 2 (September 1988), pp. 286–327.

Takagi, Keizo, "Rise of Land Prices in Japan: The Determination Mechanism and the Effect of Taxation System," *Bank of Japan Monetary and Economic Studies*, Vol. 7 (August 1989), pp. 93–139.

Ueda, Kazuo, "Are Japanese Stock Prices Too High?" *Journal of the Japanese and International Economies*, Vol. 4 (December 1990), pp. 351–70.

VII   Asset Prices, Financial Liberalization, and Inflation in Japan

Alexander W. Hoffmaister and Garry J. Schinasi

During 1986–93, asset prices in Japan moved through a dramatic and broadly symmetric cycle. Land values doubled, and corporate equity values tripled; these increases were followed by almost equal declines. At the same time, consumer price inflation remained relatively low—compared with inflation in other industrial countries and with inflation in Japan in the late 1970s and early 1980s. Because the asset price cycle in Japan has been costly in terms of lost output and financial distress, it would be useful to identify the factors that caused these dramatic asset price movements. An important unanswered question is why the sharp increases in asset prices and private indebtedness were allowed to persist; that is, why these developments were perceived as sustainable, rather than as manifestations of inflationary pressures.

One explanation that has received some attention is that the asset price inflation could not be forecast ex ante on the basis of available macroeconomic or other fundamental economic information. This characterization has been likened to a "bubble" phenomenon—a label that is adopted here for brevity—and has been interpreted to mean that the dramatic asset price increases were not closely related to fundamental economic factors. An alternative explanation that has not been examined is that there was a "regime switch" in the mid-1980s—the result of financial market reform and other structural changes—that made it difficult to accurately interpret economic and policy developments at the time. The structural changes in financial markets and in the tax treatment of real estate and equity investment in the 1980s, for example, might have been construed, ex ante, as justifying a sustainable re-evaluation of asset values relative to a basket of consumption goods. From this perspective, the asset price cycle initially might have been perceived as being driven by economic fundamentals; later in the process, the structural changes made it difficult to properly assess the stance of macroeconomic policies.

The evaluation of these alternative hypotheses is not a matter of merely academic or historical interest. If the asset price inflation was indeed a bubble, then there was little that could or should have been done to prevent or eliminate the sharp fluctuations in the asset price cycle, except to send a strong (monetary) signal early in the process that further asset market speculation would ultimately be very costly to speculators. By contrast, the regime-switch hypothesis leaves open at least two related possibilities: macroeconomic policy inadvertently fueled the asset price inflation; and the monetary policy framework in use at the time was inadequate for assessing the stance of policy and its influence on the real economy. If this second hypothesis is correct, then lessons may be drawn from the recent asset price cycle for conducting macroeconomic policy in the 1990s.

This section examines the relationship between macroeconomic variables and asset price inflation in the 1980s. The focus is on land price inflation, rather than on stock price movements; although stock prices are notoriously difficult to model empirically, real estate prices generally move in response to changes in fundamental economic factors, including the business cycle and monetary factors. This section also examines several related questions. (1) Was there a structural break in the way monetary factors, in particular, affected asset prices in the 1980s? (2) Did monetary factors contribute in important ways to asset price inflation in the 1980s? (3) What accounted for the divergent behavior of asset prices and consumer prices? (4) Is there evidence supporting the view that the effects of monetary factors were heavily concentrated in asset markets rather than in goods markets?

The next part of the section briefly reviews the relevant asset price and balance sheet developments and then examines in more detail the alternative hypotheses and important unresolved issues regarding the asset price cycle in Japan. This is followed by an attempt to quantify the extent to which macroeconomic factors, and in particular monetary factors, influenced the land price cycle in the late 1980s and to provide evidence about the regime switch and the other issues. Finally, the empirical results are summarized. An appendix briefly examines the time-series properties of the data and other statistical issues.

Key Developments and Issues

Because the important facts characterizing the asset price cycle in Japan have been examined in detail in previous studies, only the salient features of these adjustments are highlighted here.[1]

---

[1] Asset price and balance sheet adjustments occurred in other industrial countries—including the United States, the United Kingdom, the Nordic countries, Australia, and New Zealand, and have been examined in detail in previous issues of the IMF's *World Economic Outlook*; see also Schinasi and Hargraves (1993), which synthesizes this work. Adjustments in Japan have been described in fuller detail in Hoffmaister and Schinasi (1994).

Chart 7-1. Urban Land and Stock Prices

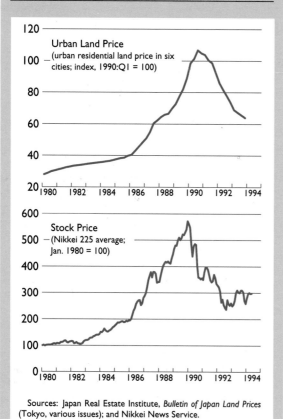

Sources: Japan Real Estate Institute, *Bulletin of Japan Land Prices* (Tokyo, various issues); and Nikkei News Service.

Asset Price and Balance Sheet Adjustments

As earlier mentioned, between 1985 and 1990 land prices in Japan doubled, and equity prices tripled. The average price of residential land in large urban centers rose 13 percent annually between 1985 and 1990, and equity prices rose 31 percent annually over the same period (Chart 7-1).

The turnaround in asset prices coincided with a change in the stance of monetary policy in early 1990. From its peak in 1990, the average price of land in the six largest Japanese cities declined by 36 percent through the end of 1993 (an average annual decline of about 14 percent). Likewise, equity prices (as measured by the Nikkei 225) plunged from a high of nearly 39,000 in February 1990 to a low of about 14,000 in August 1992; the stock market then rebounded and traded in a price range between 18,000 and 21,500 in the first half of 1994.

The sharp asset price adjustments were accompanied by equally dramatic changes in private sector balance sheets. Total private sector indebtedness expanded quite rapidly in the mid- to late 1980s, both in absolute terms and relative to GDP (Chart 7-2). Liabilities of the household and business sectors expanded markedly (Chart 7-3 and Table 7-1, respectively), and in turn this growth was reflected in the rapid expansion in the banking and nonbank financial sectors.

The balance sheet expansion in the late 1980s left households, businesses, and financial institutions unusually vulnerable to the effects of a tightening of monetary conditions in early 1990. Once asset prices began to

Chart 7-2. Total Private Nonfinancial Sector Debt¹

(In percent of GDP, end of period)

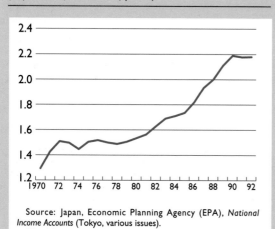

Source: Japan, Economic Planning Agency (EPA), *National Income Accounts* (Tokyo, various issues).
¹Total financial liabilities of the private nonfinancial sectors less trade credits.

Chart 7-3. Household Sector Balance Sheet

(In percent of disposable income)

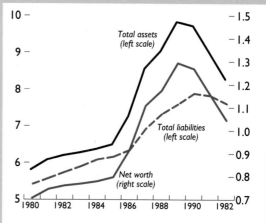

Source: Japan, EPA, *National Income Accounts* (Tokyo, various issues).

Table 7-1. Selected Indicators of Financial Balance[1]

	1970–74	1975–79	1980–84	1985	1986	1987	1988	1989	1990
Household assets	5.23	4.96	6.15	6.49	7.26	8.55	9.03	9.82	9.70
Household liabilities	0.62	0.67	0.82	0.89	0.92	1.01	1.07	1.12	1.16
Household net worth	4.61	4.29	5.32	5.61	6.34	7.54	7.95	8.71	8.54
Business assets	3.48	3.52	3.76	3.85	4.19	4.75	5.04	5.38	5.07
Business liabilities	1.91	1.90	1.94	1.98	2.00	2.12	2.16	2.17	2.23
Business net worth	1.57	1.61	1.82	1.88	2.20	2.63	2.88	3.21	2.85
Business net interest payments	49.32	63.06	53.63	46.67	44.35	40.81	38.72	40.94	49.14
Business debt-equity ratio	2.52	2.70	2.35	2.01	1.42	1.26	0.98	0.78	1.26

Source: Japan, Economic Planning Agency (EPA), *National Income Accounts* (Tokyo, various issues).
[1]Household data as a percent of disposable income; the business sector is defined as the nonfinancial corporate sector as a percent of GDP, except for the debt-equity ratio and business interest payments, which are in percent of available income.

decline, the asset sides of private sector balance sheets deteriorated sharply, leaving many private sector agents with highly leveraged positions. Moreover, the very deep and prolonged recession and the associated decline in disposable incomes and profits made it difficult for households and businesses to meet existing obligations and at the same time maintain their spending levels. As a result, both consumer expenditures and investment outlays were constrained, as an increasing share of income was devoted to servicing existing debt levels and to reducing debt to more normal levels.

Reflecting these adjustment efforts, the private sector's ratio of debt to GDP leveled off and then declined slightly through the end of 1992 (the last year for which there are data). Experience in other countries suggests that further downward adjustments are likely to occur in the period ahead—in both the household and business sectors. Households have reduced debt levels somewhat, and their net wealth has clearly been affected by the asset price deflation. Similarly, businesses have been more conscious of their leverage ratios and have pared back their debt ratios. The most difficult adjustments in the period ahead are likely to be in the financial sector.

Alternative Explanations and the Role of Monetary Factors

An important unresolved question about the asset price cycle in Japan is why the sharp increases in asset prices and private indebtedness were taken for something other than a manifestation of inflationary pressures created by overexpansionary macroeconomic policies.[2] One possible explanation, which has been supported by empirical studies, is that there was a large, unexplained bubble compo-

nent to the sharp and prolonged rises in both land and equity prices in Japan. For example, simulations below, based on a single-equation model of asset prices and using data during the period 1970:Q1–1984:Q4 show that the information available through 1985—the beginning of the asset price cycle—was not sufficient to accurately forecast the sharp rise in land prices. This conclusion holds even when the actual future values of the explanatory variables (other than the lagged dependent variable) over the forecasting period were used in the simulations. Although this exercise cannot statistically verify or falsify the existence of a bubble component in asset prices, it does forcefully illustrate how difficult it would have been in the mid-1980s to pinpoint the forces driving asset prices in the early stages of the inflation cycle.

An unexplored alternative explanation is that the asset price movements were driven by economic fundamentals, but that the confluence of structural changes in financial markets and expansionary macroeconomic policies made it difficult to interpret accurately the sharp and persistent increases in asset prices. In Japan, there were many significant developments in the early 1980s—such as the structural changes in financial markets and the tax treatment of real estate and equity investment—that might have altered in fundamental ways the relationships between macroeconomic variables and asset prices.[3] These

---

[2] For an analysis of this question, see Schinasi (1994).

[3] Extensive reform measures since 1984 have included liberalization of interest rates on deposits; the easing of restrictions on large time deposits, certificates of deposit (CDs), and money market certificates; and the introduction of markets for commercial paper, futures and options, and offshore transactions. Recent legislative reforms have further lowered barriers between banking and securities brokerage, permitting banks to establish subsidiaries that provide brokerage services and allowing securities firms to establish banking subsidiaries. In addition, tax provisions created incentives for the construction of apartment houses and condominiums, and changes in the capital gains treatment of real estate transactions encouraged upgrade purchases.

structural changes, which could have been perceived as raising the demand for assets, may have provided reasonable rationalization for believing that assets—in particular, real estate and corporate equities—were undervalued relative to consumption goods. In the initial stages of the boom in asset values, therefore, it was not unreasonable to continue to maintain the stance of monetary policy and, in effect, acquiesce to the rapid run-up in the relative price of real estate values and other asset prices.

In hindsight, a working hypothesis for understanding the dramatic asset price developments is that the prevailing monetary policy framework, together with dramatic changes in financial structures, monetary transmission mechanisms, and other important structural changes, made it difficult to distinguish sustainable adjustments in asset prices from unsustainable price increases (see Schinasi (1994)). In the initial stages of the increase in asset prices in Japan, it was presumed that the asset price increases were adjustments in relative prices in response to fundamental structural changes—including asset-market-specific tax reforms. As a result, there was a prolonged period during which inflationary pressures accumulated. Moreover, the combination of real, financial, and institutional structural changes in Japan created an environment in which inflationary pressures were channeled to, and concentrated and recycled in, asset markets for a prolonged period.[4]

Casual Empirical Evidence and Unresolved Issues

There is strong support for the concentration hypothesis. First, Japan entered the 1980s with a highly regulated financial system, which was then liberalized rapidly: ceilings on deposit interest rates were liberalized in the early 1980s; Japanese nonbank financial institutions were allowed to compete with established banks; foreign financial institutions were allowed to enter the market; and new financial instruments were allowed. In this new competitive environment there were incentives to venture into new markets—in particular, real estate markets—as

traditional borrowers shifted into other forms of financial intermediation. All of these changes led to a financial environment in which bank balance sheets were adjusting rapidly and in which both bank credit and deposits were expanding rapidly.[5] During this kind of rapid change—which was occurring in many other industrial countries as well—it was difficult to judge accurately the stance of monetary policy.[6]

Second, growth in both the monetary aggregate, M2 + CDs, and the credit aggregate, total private credit, remained very high throughout most of the 1980s. Moreover, growth in both of these financial aggregates exceeded growth in real GDP by a fairly wide margin, representing potential inflationary pressure. The difference between this "money gap" and inflation averaged $3\frac{1}{4}$ percent of GDP a year, and the difference between the "credit gap" and inflation averaged $3\frac{3}{4}$ percent of GDP a year in the 1980s (Chart 7-4). To obtain estimates of the potential "overhang" of the money stock or the stock of credit relative to the national accounts measures of economic activity, the year-by-year gaps should be accumulated, and this suggests a considerable overhang.

Third, and in strong support of the concentration hypothesis, the dramatic asset price adjustments in the 1980s did not initially pass through to goods markets in Japan, as they had in the 1970s (Chart 7-5). In most other countries that experienced asset price inflation, increases in the consumer price index (and the GDP deflator) did reflect the underlying inflationary pressures that were present, albeit in some cases with a long delay; by contrast, in Japan inflation (measured by the GDP deflator) did not rise significantly in the 1980s and did not fully reflect the demand pressures that were present in the real estate and corporate equity markets. This represented a departure from patterns that prevailed in the 1970s, when inflationary pressures tended to raise asset prices initially and were then transmitted relatively rapidly to goods prices. In the 1980s, by contrast, conventional measures of inflation, such as those based on consumer price indices or GDP deflators, remained relatively low during most of the period in which asset prices were rising at double-digit rates. That goods prices did not rise commensurately with asset prices provided some confirmation for the initial judgment that the asset price increases were sustainable.

When viewed together, these factors—structural change in the financial sector, money and credit growth in excess of GDP, and a breakdown in the relationship between asset and goods prices—suggest that monetary factors played a key role in the asset price cycle in the late 1980s, that there was a shift in the transmission of

---

[4] The concentration hypothesis is that in many industrial countries, including Japan, the confluence of macroeconomic policies, financial liberalization, and other structural changes created an environment in which excess liquidity and credit were channeled to specific groups active in asset markets, including large financial and nonfinancial institutions, high-income earners, and wealthy individuals. These groups responded to the economic incentives associated with the structural changes and borrowed heavily to accumulate assets in global markets—such as real estate, corporate equities, art, and precious commodities. Apparently, the excess credit was recycled in asset markets several times over. The structural changes that occurred in Japan are detailed in the preceding footnote. For a brief but more general discussion of the reasons that inflationary pressures may have been concentrated in asset markets, see Schinasi and Hargraves (1993, pp. 18–20).

[5] For further details see Hargraves, Schinasi, and Weisbrod (1993).
[6] For example, see Bank for International Settlements (1984 and 1986).

Chart 7-4. Money, Debt, and Inflation
(In percent)

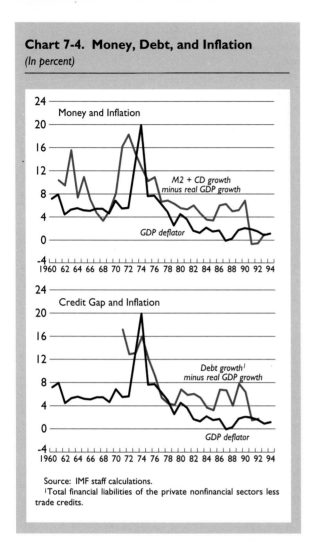

Source: IMF staff calculations.
[1]Total financial liabilities of the private nonfinancial sectors less trade credits.

Chart 7-5. Asset Prices and GDP Deflator
(In percent a year)

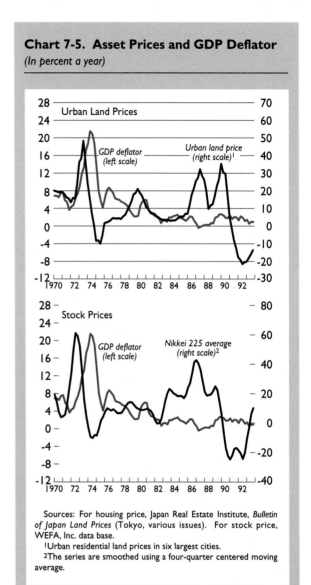

Sources: For housing price, Japan Real Estate Institute, *Bulletin of Japan Land Prices* (Tokyo, various issues). For stock price, WEFA, Inc. data base.
[1]Urban residential land prices in six largest cities.
[2]The series are smoothed using a four-quarter centered moving average.

monetary policy to inflation between the 1970s and the 1980s, and that, as a result, inflationary pressures may have been concentrated in asset markets.

A Multiequation Model of Land Prices and Inflation

Although previous studies have tried to examine the causes of these sharp adjustments in Japan, most of the issues discussed above, with few exceptions, have not been examined empirically or tested.[7] This part of the

section attempts to provide some empirical evidence on these important issues.

A Vector-Autoregression Model

To examine these issues empirically, this subsection provides estimates of a standard vector autoregression (VAR) (see Sims (1980)). Previous studies have used a single-equation approach, which requires strong assumptions about the dynamic relationships among variables and which ignores the fact that the explanatory variables are not exogenous. VAR allows for the exploration of empirical regularities and relationships with a minimum of assumptions; it also allows for the determination of the dynamic structure of relationships. A drawback of

---

[7] One exception is Samiei and Schinasi (1994), which demonstrates that monetary factors have been an important determinant of land price inflation in Japan during the period 1970–92. In addition, monetary factors were more important in the 1980s than in the 1970s—suggesting a shift in the monetary transmission process.

making fewer assumptions is a loss of specificity about the underlying structural relationships among the variables in the system.[8]

Land price inflation in Japan is assumed to be determined by several factors within the context of a more general macroeconomic system. These include: monetary and financial conditions (that is, interest rates and other measures of monetary stance); the general condition of the Japanese economy (that is, its position in the business cycle); and inflation. Because the complexity of a VAR system increases dramatically as the number of variables in the system increases, the equation system focuses on five variables, which are allowed to be jointly determined: land price inflation, consumer price inflation, the output gap, a policy-determined interest rate, and the growth rate of a policy-related financial aggregate (either a monetary or credit aggregate).[9] The variables are defined as follows:

r = call money rate
m = growth in M2 + CDs, or growth in total private credit
y = real GDP output gap
π_L = land price inflation
π = consumer price inflation.

With $X_t' = (r_t, m_t, y_t, \pi_{Lt}, \pi_t)$—where a prime (′) indicates the transpose operator—the basic model to be estimated is:

$$X_t = \sum_{i=1}^{4} A_i X_{t-i} + u_t,$$

where the A_i are (5 × 5) matrices of parameters to be estimated. That is, each of the five variables in the equation system is assumed to be determined by four lagged values of each variable in the system, including its own lagged values.[10] The errors are assumed to be identically and independently distributed, with zero means and constant variances and covariances.

The estimated VAR does not provide estimates of structural parameters, but it does provide *unconstrained* estimates of the relationships among the variables in the system. The information provided by VAR can be represented in three useful and related forms: estimates of the autoregressive parameters (and the associated test statistics), which relate each variable to the other system variables; variance decompositions, which provide estimates of the share of the variance of each variable that is explained by the other variables in the system; and impulse response functions, which indicate how the variables respond to various orthogonal shocks.[11] In examining land price inflation, for example, the estimated autoregressive parameters on monetary factors can be jointly tested for their statistical significance; the variance decomposition can be examined to determine the importance of monetary innovations (that is, monetary policy changes) in determining the variation in land prices; and the impulse response function can be used to examine the reaction of land price inflation to a monetary innovation.

To construct the variance decompositions and the impulse response functions, the variables in the system must be ordered according to their contemporaneous exogeneity (see Sims (1980)). The following ordering is adopted initially: the call money rate; either the monetary or credit aggregate; business cycle conditions; property prices; and, finally, general inflationary pressures. Later, to check for robustness, the order is changed to see if the empirical results are sensitive to the original ordering of the variables.

The initial ordering of variables is not arbitrary, however. The call money rate is assumed to be the most contemporaneously exogenous variable in the system because the Bank of Japan uses the call money rate as its operating instrument in the short run. This does not mean that the call money rate is assumed to be unaffected by the other variables in the system, such as business cycle conditions; but innovations in the call money rate in any given quarter affect all of the other variables in the system, whereas innovations in other variables do not affect the call money rate in the same quarter. Innovations in the call money rate are assumed to affect directly the banks' cost of funds, which in turn affects monetary conditions by altering the behavior of financial institutions and their balance sheets. Monetary conditions are represented in the model either by growth on the liability side of the banking system (growth in M2 + CDs) or the asset side of the banking system (growth in private credit). Innovations in both the call money rate and the financial aggregate are then presumed to affect the general condition of the economy, as summarized in the output gap; and innovations in monetary conditions and the output gap are presumed to affect land price inflation, and so on.

Empirical Results

Using the estimated VAR parameters, variance decompositions, and impulse response functions, several issues are examined. (1) Was there a regime switch in the 1980s

---

[8] A disadvantage of the standard VAR approach is that the underlying behavioral relationships that may exist cannot be identified; the estimated parameters are reduced-form estimates, and care must be exercised in interpreting the implications of the estimated equations.

[9] Other variables that were included are a measure of fiscal policy and alternative measures of the monetary stance, such as the exchange rate, but they did not alter the results in important (or even notable) ways.

[10] The parameters are estimated using ordinary least squares, which is in this case the full-information maximum-likelihood estimator. See Appendix 7-1 for the determination of the lag length.

[11] In a standard VAR, the orthogonal innovations are obtained from the Choleski decomposition of the covariance matrix.

compared with the 1970s? (2) What role did monetary factors play in the land price inflation in the 1980s? (3) Did the process of consumer price inflation also change? (4) Were the effects of monetary factors more concentrated in asset prices, and less concentrated in consumer prices, in the 1980s compared with the 1970s?

Was There a Regime Switch in the 1980s?

Because of the financial changes that occurred in Japan in the 1980s, it is unlikely that the structure of an estimated model would remain stable during the period 1970–93—this is probably what accounts for the inability of models estimated through 1985 to predict asset prices accurately in the mid- to late 1980s and early 1990s. Unfortunately, it is difficult to construct variables that would allow for precise estimates of the effects of financial liberalization, for example, or changes in the tax treatment of real estate investment.

The alternative strategy followed here is to split the sample into two periods, with the intention of capturing the shift in underlying regimes: one period in which the financial system in Japan was tightly regulated, and a second period in which the financial system had more or less been liberalized. Although it is not possible to determine with precision when the Japanese economy entered the liberalized regime, the shift is treated as having occurred in the period 1982–84, for two reasons. First, although liberalization began well before 1982–84, the full effects of financial liberalization would take some time to take hold. Second, the global economy experienced a prolonged recession in the early 1980s. To prevent these transitional factors from affecting the statistical tests, several breakpoints, beginning in 1983 and ending in 1985, were examined.

By comparing the residuals of the model estimated over the entire sample with those estimated over the various subsamples defined by the breakpoints (that is, by performing likelihood ratio tests) it is possible to test the hypothesis that the model parameters were constant over the entire sample period. The various likelihood ratio tests reject the hypothesis of parameter constancy for all of the alternative sample periods in the 1980s that were tried (see Appendix 7-1). For example, when the liberalized regime was assumed to begin in the first quarter of 1984, the F-test of a structural break is significant at the 9 percent level when M2 + CDs is used as the financial aggregate and at the 1 percent level when private credit is used as the financial aggregate (see Table 7-1). As discussed in the next subsection, this evidence of a structural change in the VAR system is supported by empirical evidence provided in the estimated equation for land price inflation and is consistent with the results reported in Samiei and Schinasi (1994). The remainder of this subsection documents the changes in the estimated land price and consumer price inflation equations, which were estimated over two fixed sample periods:

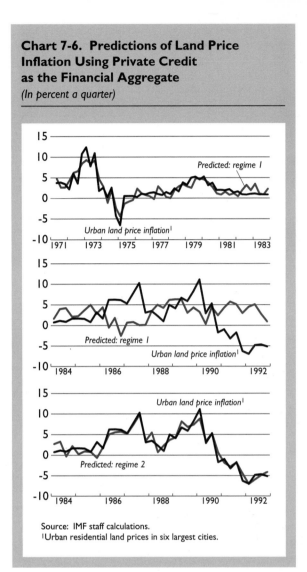

Chart 7-6. Predictions of Land Price Inflation Using Private Credit as the Financial Aggregate
(In percent a quarter)

Source: IMF staff calculations.
[1]Urban residential land prices in six largest cities.

the "regulated" regime during 1970:Q1–1983:Q4 and the "liberalized" regime during 1984:Q1–1993:Q4.

To illustrate the nature of the regime switch, Charts 7-6 and 7-7 present a comparison of model predictions (static simulations) of land price inflation and consumer price inflation, respectively, using the estimated land price and consumer price equations. The top panel of Chart 7-6 presents the within-sample predictions of the land price inflation equation when its parameters are estimated in the first period, 1970:Q1–1983:Q4. Despite the wide variation in land price inflation in the regulated regime, the within-sample predictions indicate that the model describes the movement in land price inflation reasonably well in the 1970s.[12] Using the parameters

---

[12] The next subsection presents dynamic simulations of the land price equation using projected values of the lagged dependent variable.

Chart 7-7. Predictions of Consumer Price Inflation Using Private Credit as the Financial Aggregate

(In percent a quarter)

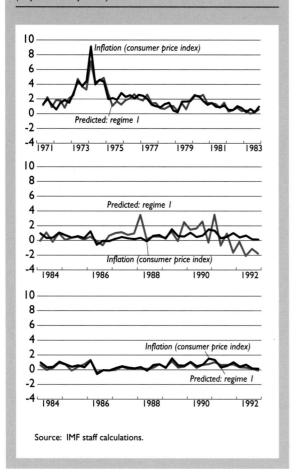

Source: IMF staff calculations.

estimated in the regulated regime, the model's out-of-sample predictions of land price inflation were generated for the liberalized regime, using the actual observations on the explanatory variables, 1984:Q1–1993:Q4, including the lagged dependent variable (see the middle panel). The model estimated in the regulated regime fails to predict land price inflation accurately in the liberalized regime. By contrast, as shown in the bottom panel, the within-sample predictions of the land price inflation equation estimated in the liberalized regime tracks actual land price inflation reasonably well. Note that casual empiricism (see Chart 7-6) suggests that there was a fairly wide variation in land price inflation in both regimes, suggesting that the structural break is not attributable *directly* to a shift in the behavior of the land price data.

A similar structural break is apparent in the consumer price inflation time series (see Chart 7-7). The parameters estimated in the regulated regime describe quite well the within-sample movements in consumer price inflation, but they do not provide an accurate description of consumer price movements in the liberalized regime, again suggesting a structural break. The bottom panel of this chart shows that when the model's parameters are re-estimated using the data in the liberalized regime, the model describes consumer price developments reasonably well.

The Role of Monetary Factors in Land Price Inflation

An important feature of the estimated land price equation is that monetary factors (the call money rate and either the money or credit aggregate) together played an important role in the determination of land price inflation; moreover, credit and interest rates together were significantly more important in explaining land price inflation in the 1980s than in the 1970s. This is clear from the marginal significance levels of the estimated coefficients (Tables 7-2 and 7-3), from the implied variance decompositions (Tables 7-4 and 7-5), and from the estimated impulse response functions (discussed below).

Variance decompositions, which quantify the percentage contribution of each variable to the variation in land price inflation, are shown in Table 7-4. The share of the variation in land price inflation accounted for by monetary factors increases significantly in the second period, regardless of whether M2 + CDs or private credit is assumed to be the relevant financial aggregate. With M2 + CDs as the financial aggregate, the contribution of monetary factors to the variation in the land price inflation increases from a share of 50 percent in the 1970s to over 80 percent in the 1980s; with total private credit as the financial aggregate, the contribution of monetary factors to the variation in the land price inflation increases from a share of 35 percent in the 1970s to 75 percent in the 1980s. Note that when M2 + CDs is assumed to be the financial aggregate, the contribution of the call money rate becomes negligible in the second period; in contrast, the contribution of the call money rate remains important and increases when credit is assumed to be the financial aggregate. Finally, note that the output gap accounted for almost one fourth of the variation in land price inflation in the 1970s, regardless of the choice of financial aggregate. In the 1980s, however, the output gap accounted for less than 10 percent of the variation in land price inflation because of the dominance of monetary factors.

Variance decompositions are sensitive to the ordering of the variables according to their presumed exogeneity. One way of examining the robustness of a variable's contribution is to alter the order of the variables. When the monetary variables were placed last in the ordering (that is, assuming that monetary factors were affected by

Table 7-2. F-Tests for Lagged Values of Explanatory Variables: Broad Money (M2 + CDs)
(Significance levels are in parentheses)

	Land Price Inflation		Consumer Price Inflation	
	1970–83	1984–92	1970–83	1984–92
Call money rate	1.50 (0.24)	0.30 (0.87)	2.10 (0.12)	2.20 (0.12)
M2 + CDs	7.10 (0.00)	2.60 (0.08)	3.50 (0.02)	1.00 (0.45)
Output gap	3.20 (0.03)	0.60 (0.69)	0.90 (0.47)	1.10 (0.40)
Land price inflation	0.60 (0.69)	1.90 (0.17)	1.20 (0.35)	0.20 (0.93)
Consumer price inflation	2.60 (0.06)	1.10 (0.39)	3.60 (0.02)	1.40 (0.29)
Memorandum				
R^2 (coefficient of determination)	0.88	0.88	0.87	0.65
$\bar{R}^2$ (adjusted R^2)	0.77	0.69	0.76	0.12
Observations	51.00	39.00	51.00	39.00
Degrees of freedom	27.00	15.00	27.00	15.00
Standard error	1.50	2.60	0.75	0.43

Source: IMF staff calculations.

contemporaneous innovations in the other variables), the contribution of M2 + CDs to the variation in land price inflation declined in the 1980s, whereas that of private credit increased substantially in the 1980s (see Table 7-5). Thus, the contribution of M2 + CDs to the variation in land price inflation in the 1980s is not robust, but that of total private credit is. The changes in the contribution of the call money rate and the output gap noted above in the discussion of the initial ordering of variables are also robust.

One interpretation of the estimated land price equations is that there was a change in the transmission of monetary factors to real estate markets in the 1980s. Under this interpretation, the change in the transmission process led to two important structural changes: first, bank credit (bank assets) played a more important role in the 1980s than in the 1970s; second, bank credit played a more important role in determining land price inflation than did bank deposits (bank liabilities). This may imply that bank credit became a more important indicator of inflationary pressures in the 1980s. If this structural change is sustained, it will have important implications for the conduct of monetary policy in the 1990s.

To assess further the relative importance of the transmission processes of money versus credit, and to examine how well the estimated equations track the actual path of land price inflation in the 1980s, Chart 7-8 presents

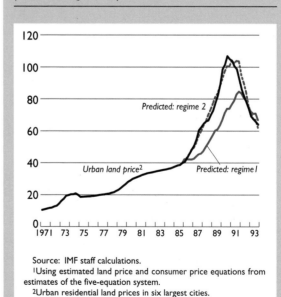

Chart 7-8. Dynamic Simulations Using Two-Equation Subsystem and M2 + CDs as the Financial Aggregate[1]
(Index, 1990:Q1 = 100)

Source: IMF staff calculations.
[1]Using estimated land price and consumer price equations from estimates of the five-equation system.
[2]Urban residential land prices in six largest cities.

**Table 7-3. *F*-Tests for Lagged Values of Explanatory Variables:
Credit Consistent with National Accounts**
(Significance levels are in parentheses)

	Land Price Inflation		Consumer Price Inflation	
	1970–83	1984–92	1970–83	1984–92
Call money rate	0.70	1.20	0.80	2.60
	(0.60)	(0.35)	(0.53)	(0.09)
Private credit	2.10	5.40	2.60	2.90
	(0.11)	(0.01)	(0.06)	(0.07)
Output gap	2.20	1.20	1.60	1.90
	(0.10)	(0.34)	(0.21)	(0.17)
Land price inflation	0.30	1.80	1.90	1.00
	(0.86)	(0.18)	(0.13)	(0.46)
Consumer price inflation	1.40	2.90	5.40	2.70
	(0.27)	(0.07)	(0.00)	(0.08)
Memorandum				
R^2 (coefficient of determination)	0.88	0.95	0.94	0.91
$\overline{R}^2$ (adjusted)	0.64	0.80	0.74	0.53
Observations	51.00	36.00	51.00	36.00
Degrees of freedom	27.00	12.00	27.00	12.00
Standard error	1.90	2.00	0.79	0.47

Source: IMF staff calculations.

**Table 7-4. Variance Decompositions for the Land Price and Consumer
Price Equations: Monetary Variables First in the Ordering**
(Percent of total variance)[1]

	Interest Rate	M2 + CDs	Output Gap	Land Price	Consumer Prices	Monetary Combined
Land price equation						
First period	19	30	22	18	10	50
Second period	3	80	6	4	8	83
Consumer price equation						
First period	12	38	13	9	27	50
Second period	27	38	10	2	24	64

	Interest Rate	Credit	Output Gap	Land Price	Consumer Prices	Monetary Combined
Land price equation						
First period	22	14	23	28	13	35
Second period	27	48	8	11	6	75
Consumer price equation						
First period	18	15	14	16	36	34
Second period	25	35	19	10	12	60

Source: IMF staff calculations.
[1]Percent of the total variance at the twentieth quarter (that is, in the long run).

Table 7-5. Variance Decompositions for the Land Price and Consumer Price Equations: Monetary Variables Last in the Ordering
(Percent of total variance)[1]

	Output Gap	Land Price	Consumer Prices	Interest Rate	M2 + CDs	Monetary Combined
Land price equation						
First period	13	22	12	25	28	53
Second period	3	38	37	3	19	22
Consumer price equation						
First period	9	13	31	16	32	48
Second period	12	22	48	8	10	18

	Output Gap	Land Price	Consumer Prices	Interest Rate	Credit	Monetary Combined
Land price equation						
First period	20	31	20	18	10	28
Second period	15	13	13	26	33	59
Consumer price equation						
First period	10	19	43	14	15	28
Second period	29	9	18	17	27	45

Source: IMF staff calculations.
[1]Percent of the total variance at the twentieth quarter (that is, in the long run).

Chart 7-9. Dynamic Simulations Using Two-Equation Subsystem and Private Credit as the Financial Aggregate: Urban Land Prices[1]
(Index, 1990:Q1 = 100)

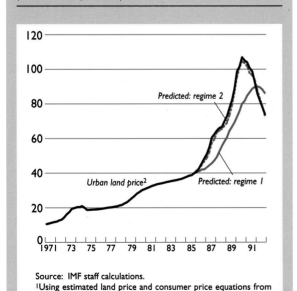

Source: IMF staff calculations.
[1]Using estimated land price and consumer price equations from estimates of the five-equation system.
[2]Urban residential land prices in six largest cities.

dynamic simulations of the land price equation using M2 + CDs as the financial aggregate, and Chart 7-9 presents dynamic simulations for the model using total private credit as the financial aggregate. The lines labeled "regime 1" represent the dynamic simulation of the model when the parameters are estimated over the regulated regime, and the lines labeled "regime 2" represent the dynamic simulation of the model when the parameters are estimated in the liberalized regime.

The simulations are "dynamic" in the sense that the path of inflation is simulated using the forecasted values of the lagged dependent variable, but actual data are used for the other explanatory variables.[13] These dynamic simulations provide information about whether the land price inflation could have been accurately forecasted by the model had the evolution of the monetary policy variables and the output gap been known.

---

[13] These simulations use actual data for nonprice variables (the call money rate; the financial aggregate, either M2 + CDs or private credit; and the output gap), but projected values for the lagged price variables. To examine the explanatory power of the lagged dependent variable, the simulation was run assuming coefficients of zero on lagged values of land price inflation. For the equation using total private credit, the only difference in the simulation was that land prices overshot the peak for about two quarters—and by about 10–15 percent—and then turned downward and followed a path parallel to the one presented in Chart 7-9; this is what is suggested by the variance decompositions presented in Tables 7-4 and 7-5, in which the contribution of lagged values in land price inflation to the total variation of land price inflation was less than 10 percent.

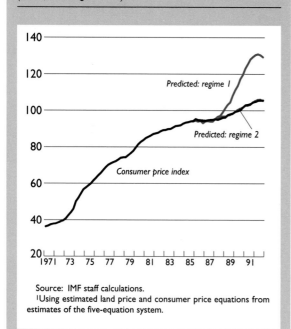

Chart 7-10. Dynamic Simulations Using Two-Equation Subsystem and Private Credit as the Financial Aggregate: Consumer Prices[1]

(Index, 1990:Q1 = 100)

Source: IMF staff calculations.
[1]Using estimated land price and consumer price equations from estimates of the five-equation system.

ship between consumer price inflation and the other variables in the estimated system. In the 1970s, lagged values of M2 + CDs, consumer prices, and the call money rate were fairly important variables in the estimated consumer price inflation equation, and these determinants together explained a very high share of the overall variation of consumer price inflation in the first subsample period. In the 1980s, however, these marginal contributions declined, and the explanatory variables together have very little explanatory power—as represented by the adjusted coefficient of determination, $\bar{R}^2$.

In contrast, when private credit is used as the financial aggregate, the marginal significance of lagged values of private credit and the call money rate improve, and that of lagged values of consumer price inflation declines. In addition, with private credit as the aggregate, the marginal significance of the output gap is greater than when broad money is the financial aggregate. Overall, the equation with private credit holds up fairly well, and monetary factors (the call money rate and private credit) were more important in determining goods-price inflation in the 1980s than in the 1970s.[15]

As discussed earlier, the hypothesis that there was a structural break in the early to mid-1980s in the model is illustrated by the static simulations of the consumer price inflation equation (see Chart 7-7). Chart 7-10 shows two dynamic simulations for consumer prices. The line labeled "regime 1" represents a dynamic simulation of the consumer price inflation equation using coefficients estimated in the regulated data regime, whereas "regime 2" uses the model coefficients estimated using the data in the liberalized data regime. These simulations clearly show that, given the actual evolution of the call money rate, credit growth, and the output gap, the model estimated over the regulated regime would predict greater inflation on average than either the model estimated over the liberalized data regime *or* actual consumer price developments.

The Concentration of Monetary Shocks in Land Prices

Taken together, the "dynamic" simulations for both price equations suggest that the concentration hypothesis discussed earlier cannot easily be rejected. The five-equation model estimated over the liberalized data regime clearly suggests that the actual evolution of monetary

As the charts show, regardless of the financial aggregate used for estimation, the parameters estimated using data in the liberalized regime perform very well and are significantly better than the parameters estimated using data in the regulated regime. Indeed, the simulations of regime 1 in each case suggest that fundamental macroeconomic variables could not explain very well the land price inflation—implying that it might be a bubble. Also note that, although growth in M2 + CDs performs reasonably well as a financial aggregate, growth in total private credit clearly dominates the monetary aggregate, which confirms the information contained in the variance decompositions.[14]

The Consumer Price Inflation Equation

An important additional manifestation of the apparent regime shift was a breakdown in the 1980s in the relation-

___

[14] When full dynamic simulations are run—that is, using the estimated forecasted values of all of the explanatory variables, including estimated values of r, m, y, π_L, and π—the models do not perform very well. But as the "dynamic" simulations show, this is largely because of the errors in forecasting r, m, and y.

___

[15] When the five-equation system was expanded to include the exchange rate as a third monetary factor, the land price equation was qualitatively unaffected; in addition, lagged values of the exchange rate made a statistically significant marginal contribution, the call money rate and the financial aggregate remained significant, and the overall fit improved. Regarding the estimated consumer price equation, the most important difference was that the contribution of monetary factors to the variation in consumer price inflation increased.

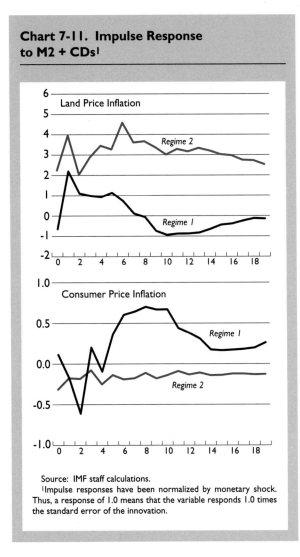

Chart 7-11. Impulse Response to M2 + CDs[1]

Source: IMF staff calculations.
[1]Impulse responses have been normalized by monetary shock. Thus, a response of 1.0 means that the variable responds 1.0 times the standard error of the innovation.

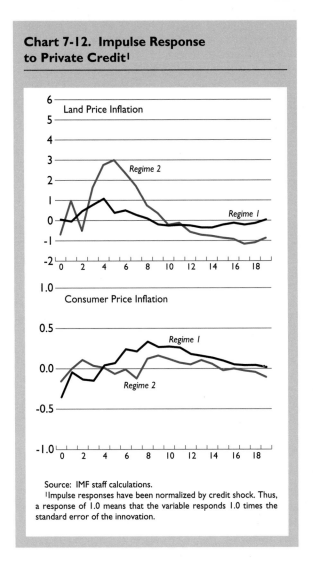

Chart 7-12. Impulse Response to Private Credit[1]

Source: IMF staff calculations.
[1]Impulse responses have been normalized by credit shock. Thus, a response of 1.0 means that the variable responds 1.0 times the standard error of the innovation.

variables in the mid- to late 1980s led to more land price inflation and less consumer price inflation than would have been predicted by the model estimated over the regulated regime.

These results imply that a money or credit shock to the equation system would lead to a concentration of inflationary pressure in land prices and not in goods prices in the liberalized data regime compared with the regulated data regime. This can be examined directly by examining the impulse response functions implicit in the estimated land price and consumer price inflation equations. The responses of land price inflation and consumer price inflation to a monetary shock and a credit shock are shown in Charts 7-11 and 7-12, respectively. The impulse response functions suggest that both monetary and credit shocks were more heavily concentrated in asset markets than in goods markets in the liberalized regime than they were in the regulated regime.

Conclusions

An important conclusion to be drawn from the preceding analyses is that movements in land price inflation in Japan in the 1980s can be explained quite well by a relatively unrestricted multiequation model that includes monetary factors, the output gap, and consumer price inflation—with monetary factors being the most important. A second important conclusion is that the hypothesis that there was no regime switch in the period 1970–93 is strongly rejected by the data. Specifically, a feature of the estimated system of equations is that the dynamic forces that determined land price and consumer price inflation in the period 1970–83 were quite different from those in 1984–93. In the second period there was a sizable increase—a doubling—in the contribution of monetary factors to the variation in land price inflation, and both land price and consumer price inflation in the second period were more affected by total private credit than by M2 + CDs. In addition, the view that inflationary pressures in the 1980s were highly concentrated in asset prices is broadly supported by the estimated model; a monetary shock (or a credit shock) leads to more land price inflation and to less consumer price inflation when the model is simulated using parameters estimated over the period 1984–93 than when the parameters are estimated over the period 1970–83. Thus, a key conclusion is that, although monetary expansion typically led to consumer price inflation before the mid-1980s, because of structural changes it has since tended to manifest itself in asset price inflation.

In sum, the empirical results suggest that financial deregulation, which took place in the late 1970s and throughout the 1980s, had an important influence in redirecting the influence of monetary factors toward asset markets.

Appendix 7-1. Vector-Autoregression Modeling

This appendix consists of three brief subsections that deal with the time-series properties of the data, the number of lags to include in the VAR model, and evidence of a structural break in the model.

Time-Series Properties

Before estimating the VAR model, the time-series properties of the different variables were examined to ensure efficient estimation. Standard unit root tests were used to determine the time-series properties of the variables. These unit root tests suggest that all the variables are stationary (Table 7-6).

The number of lags included in these tests was chosen by "testing down" for the highest significant lag. Monte Carlo simulations suggest that this selection mechanism will choose the correct number of lags as the number of observations increases (see Campbell and Perron (1991)).

The augmented Dickey-Fuller and the Phillips-Perron tests reject the presence of a unit root for all variables except for land inflation and relative land inflation. Two possible reasons can explain why these tests failed to reject the null hypothesis of a unit root for land inflation and relative land inflation. First, it is well known that these tests have low power to discriminate between a moderately high persistent series and a true unit root. Second, the tests could fail to recognize a stationary series when the series contains a break, as is the case with land price series.

Lag Length

Following Lütkepohl (1985), we have calculated the Hannan-Quinn and Schwarz test for four VAR models (Table 7-7). The first two models use M2 + CDs as the monetary aggregate, one with land price inflation and the other with relative land price inflation. The third and fourth models use credit as the monetary aggregate, one with land price inflation and the other with relative land price inflation.

The tests suggest that four lags are appropriate for all models except the model with credit and land inflation, where three lags are selected. However, for consistency in the degrees of freedom, we have chosen to estimate all four models with four lags.

Structural Breaks

To test for a structural break in the VAR model, log-likelihood ratio tests were performed. The 120 coeffi-

Table 7-6. Unit Root Tests

Series	ADF[1]	PP[2]	Critical Values[3]	
			5 percent	10 percent
Output gap	−3.15	−3.14	−3.29	−3.03
M2 + CDs	−2.87	−2.92	−3.29	−3.03
Credit	−1.58	−3.24	−3.29	−3.03
Interest rate	−3.75	−2.41	−3.29	−3.03
Inflation	−2.32	−3.58	−3.29	−3.03
Land inflation	−2.14	−2.97	−3.29	−3.03
Relative land inflation	−2.34	−2.71	−3.29	−3.03

[1]Augmented Dickey-Fuller test.
[2]Phillips-Perron test.
[3]Taken from Guilkey and Schmidt (1989, Table 1; $n = 100$).

Table 7-7. Lag Length Tests[1]

Lag	Land Inflation (1)	Land Inflation (2)	Relative Land Inflation (1)	Relative Land Inflation (2)
	M2 + CDs			
1	58.01	57.61	60.26	59.85
2	58.11	57.29	57.15	56.33
3	58.50	57.26	58.99	57.76
4	56.46*	54.82*	55.34*	53.68*
5	61.95	59.87	59.87	57.78
6	62.27	59.74	59.40	56.88
7	60.20	57.24	60.45	57.49
8	64.22	60.81	65.27	61.86
	Credit			
1	61.29	60.88	59.84	59.43
2	58.27	57.45	57.45	56.64
3	55.28*	54.04*	60.60	59.37
4	61.30	59.64	56.46*	54.80*
5	56.95	54.86	57.73	55.65
6	59.47	56.95	60.12	57.60
7	58.30	55.34	61.56	58.60
8	65.15	61.73	63.05	59.64

[1](1) and (2) correspond to the Hannan-Quinn and Schwarz tests; an asterisk (*) denotes the lag length selected.

Table 7-8. Likelihood Ratio Tests for Structural Breaks

	System with M2 + CDs		System with Credit	
	χ^2	Marginal significance	χ^2	Marginal significance
1982:Q4	150.43	0.03	185.29	—
1983:Q1	144.20	0.07	179.35	—
1983:Q2	144.37	0.06	171.03	—
1983:Q3	143.19	0.07	171.16	—
1983:Q4	141.16	0.09	173.03	—
1984:Q1	141.61	0.09	175.26	—
1984:Q2	139.33	0.11	182.55	—
1984:Q3	140.78	0.09	183.24	—
1984:Q4	141.08	0.09	188.88	—
1985:Q1	145.03	0.06	193.49	—
1985:Q2	148.49	0.04	202.04	—
1985:Q3	146.60	0.05	204.94	—
1985:Q4	160.67	—	215.47	—

cients ((5 equations × 5 variables × 4 lags) + (4 seasonal dummies × 5 equations)) of the unconstrained model were estimated over two different subsamples, while the coefficients of the constrained model were not allowed to vary and were estimated over the entire sample.

Two VAR models were tested for structural breaks (Table 7-8). The first model uses M2 + CDs as the monetary aggregate, while the second uses credit; both use land inflation as the asset price. The test results find statistically significant evidence to support the hypothesis that there was a break in the model in the early 1980s.

References

Bank for International Settlements, *Financial Innovation and Monetary Policy* (Basle, March 1984).

———, *Changes in Money-Market Instruments and Procedures: Objectives and Implications* (Basle, March 1986).

Campbell, John Y., and Pierre Perron, "Pitfalls and Opportunities: What Macroeconomists Should Know About Unit Roots," in *NBER Macroeconomics Annual 1991*, edited by Olivier Jean Blanchard and Stanley Fischer (Cambridge, Massachusetts: MIT Press, 1991).

Guilkey, David K., and Peter Schmidt, "Extended Tabulations for Dickey-Fuller Tests," *Economics Letters*, Vol. 31 (1989), pp. 355–57.

Hargraves, Monica, Garry J. Schinasi, and Steven R. Weisbrod, "Asset Price Inflation in the 1980s: A Flow of Funds Perspective," IMF Working Paper 93/77 (Washington, October 1993).

Hoffmaister, Alexander W., and Garry J. Schinasi, "Asset Prices, Financial Liberalization, and the Process of Inflation in Japan," IMF Working Paper 94/153 (Washington, December 1994).

International Monetary Fund, *World Economic Outlook* (Washington, various issues).

Lütkepohl, Helmut, "Comparison of Criteria for Estimating the Order of a Vector Autoregressive Process," *Journal of Time Series Analysis*, Vol. 6 (No. 1, 1985), pp. 35–52.

Samiei, Hossein, and Garry J. Schinasi, "Real Estate Price Inflation, Monetary Policy, and Expectations in the United States and Japan," IMF Working Paper 94/12 (Washington, January 1994).

Schinasi, Garry J., "Asset Prices, Monetary Policy, and the Business Cycle," IMF Paper on Policy Analysis and Assessment 94/6 (Washington, March 1994).

Schinasi, Garry J., and Monica Hargraves, "'Boom and Bust' in Asset Markets in the 1980s: Causes and Consequences," in *Staff Studies for the World Economic Outlook* (Washington: International Monetary Fund, December 1993), pp. 1–27.

Sims, Christopher, "Macroeconomics and Reality," *Econometrica*, Vol. 48 (January 1980), pp. 1–48.

Recent Occasional Papers of the International Monetary Fund

124. Saving Behavior and the Asset Price "Bubble" in Japan: Analytical Studies, edited by Ulrich Baumgartner and Guy Meredith. 1995.

123. Comprehensive Tax Reform: The Colombian Experience, edited by Parthasarathi Shome. 1995.

122. Capital Flows in the APEC Region, edited by Mohsin S. Khan and Carmen M. Reinhart. 1995.

121. Uganda: Adjustment with Growth, 1987–94, by Robert L. Sharer, Hema R. De Zoysa, and Calvin A. McDonald. 1995.

120. Economic Dislocation and Recovery in Lebanon, by Sena Eken, Paul Cashin, S. Nuri Erbas, Jose Martelino, and Adnan Mazarei. 1995.

119. Singapore: A Case Study in Rapid Development, edited by Kenneth Bercuson with a staff team comprising Robert G. Carling, Aasim M. Husain, Thomas Rumbaugh, and Rachel van Elkan. 1995.

118. Sub-Saharan Africa: Growth, Savings, and Investment, by Michael T. Hadjimichael, Dhaneshwar Ghura, Martin Mühleisen, Roger Nord, and E. Murat Uçer. 1995.

117. Resilience and Growth Through Sustained Adjustment: The Moroccan Experience, by Saleh M. Nsouli, Sena Eken, Klaus Enders, Van-Can Thai, Jörg Decressin, and Filippo Cartiglia, with Janet Bungay. 1995.

116. Improving the International Monetary System: Constraints and Possibilities, by Michael Mussa, Morris Goldstein, Peter B. Clark, Donald J. Mathieson, and Tamim Bayoumi. 1994.

115. Exchange Rates and Economic Fundamentals: A Framework for Analysis, by Peter B. Clark, Leonardo Bartolini, Tamim Bayoumi, and Steven Symansky. 1994.

114. Economic Reform in China: A New Phase, by Wanda Tseng, Hoe Ee Khor, Kalpana Kochhar, Dubravko Mihaljek, and David Burton. 1994.

113. Poland: The Path to a Market Economy, by Liam P. Ebrill, Ajai Chopra, Charalambos Christofides, Paul Mylonas, Inci Otker, and Gerd Schwartz. 1994.

112. The Behavior of Non-Oil Commodity Prices, by Eduardo Borensztein, Mohsin S. Khan, Carmen M. Reinhart, and Peter Wickham. 1994.

111. The Russian Federation in Transition: External Developments, by Benedicte Vibe Christensen. 1994.

110. Limiting Central Bank Credit to the Government: Theory and Practice, by Carlo Cottarelli. 1993.

109. The Path to Convertibility and Growth: The Tunisian Experience, by Saleh M. Nsouli, Sena Eken, Paul Duran, Gerwin Bell, and Zühtü Yücelik. 1993.

108. Recent Experiences with Surges in Capital Inflows, by Susan Schadler, Maria Carkovic, Adam Bennett, and Robert Kahn. 1993.

107. China at the Threshold of a Market Economy, by Michael W. Bell, Hoe Ee Khor, and Kalpana Kochhar with Jun Ma, Simon N'guiamba, and Rajiv Lall. 1993.

106. Economic Adjustment in Low-Income Countries: Experience Under the Enhanced Structural Adjustment Facility, by Susan Schadler, Franek Rozwadowski, Siddharth Tiwari, and David O. Robinson. 1993.

105. The Structure and Operation of the World Gold Market, by Gary O'Callaghan. 1993.

104. Price Liberalization in Russia: Behavior of Prices, Household Incomes, and Consumption During the First Year, by Vincent Koen and Steven Phillips. 1993.

103. Liberalization of the Capital Account: Experiences and Issues, by Donald J. Mathieson and Liliana Rojas-Suárez. 1993.

102. Financial Sector Reforms and Exchange Arrangements in Eastern Europe. Part I: Financial Markets and Intermediation, by Guillermo A. Calvo and Manmohan S. Kumar. Part II: Exchange Arrangements of Previously Centrally Planned Economies, by Eduardo Borensztein and Paul R. Masson. 1993.

101. Spain: Converging with the European Community, by Michel Galy, Gonzalo Pastor, and Thierry Pujol. 1993.

100. The Gambia: Economic Adjustment in a Small Open Economy, by Michael T. Hadjimichael, Thomas Rumbaugh, and Eric Verreydt. 1992.

99. Mexico: The Strategy to Achieve Sustained Economic Growth, edited by Claudio Loser and Eliot Kalter. 1992.

98. Albania: From Isolation Toward Reform, by Mario I. Blejer, Mauro Mecagni, Ratna Sahay, Richard Hides, Barry Johnston, Piroska Nagy, and Roy Pepper. 1992.

97. Rules and Discretion in International Economic Policy, by Manuel Guitián. 1992.

96. Policy Issues in the Evolving International Monetary System, by Morris Goldstein, Peter Isard, Paul R. Masson, and Mark P. Taylor. 1992.

95. The Fiscal Dimensions of Adjustment in Low-Income Countries, by Karim Nashashibi, Sanjeev Gupta, Claire Liuksila, Henri Lorie, and Walter Mahler. 1992.

94. Tax Harmonization in the European Community: Policy Issues and Analysis, edited by George Kopits. 1992.

93. Regional Trade Arrangements, by Augusto de la Torre and Margaret R. Kelly. 1992.

92. Stabilization and Structural Reform in the Czech and Slovak Federal Republic: First Stage, by Bijan B. Aghevli, Eduardo Borensztein, and Tessa van der Willigen. 1992.

91. Economic Policies for a New South Africa, edited by Desmond Lachman and Kenneth Bercuson with a staff team comprising Daudi Ballali, Robert Corker, Charalambos Christofides, and James Wein. 1992.

90. The Internationalization of Currencies: An Appraisal of the Japanese Yen, by George S. Tavlas and Yuzuru Ozeki. 1992.

89. The Romanian Economic Reform Program, by Dimitri G. Demekas and Mohsin S. Khan. 1991.

88. Value-Added Tax: Administrative and Policy Issues, edited by Alan A. Tait. 1991.

87. Financial Assistance from Arab Countries and Arab Regional Institutions, by Pierre van den Boogaerde. 1991.

86. Ghana: Adjustment and Growth, 1983–91, by Ishan Kapur, Michael T. Hadjimichael, Paul Hilbers, Jerald Schiff, and Philippe Szymczak. 1991.

85. Thailand: Adjusting to Success—Current Policy Issues, by David Robinson, Yangho Byeon, and Ranjit Teja with Wanda Tseng. 1991.

84. Financial Liberalization, Money Demand, and Monetary Policy in Asian Countries, by Wanda Tseng and Robert Corker. 1991.

83. Economic Reform in Hungary Since 1968, by Anthony R. Boote and Janos Somogyi. 1991.

82. Characteristics of a Successful Exchange Rate System, by Jacob A. Frenkel, Morris Goldstein, and Paul R. Masson. 1991.

81. Currency Convertibility and the Transformation of Centrally Planned Economies, by Joshua E. Greene and Peter Isard. 1991.

80. Domestic Public Debt of Externally Indebted Countries, by Pablo E. Guidotti and Manmohan S. Kumar. 1991.

79. The Mongolian People's Republic: Toward a Market Economy, by Elizabeth Milne, John Leimone, Franek Rozwadowski, and Padej Sukachevin. 1991.

78. Exchange Rate Policy in Developing Countries: Some Analytical Issues, by Bijan B. Aghevli, Mohsin S. Khan, and Peter J. Montiel. 1991.

77. Determinants and Systemic Consequences of International Capital Flows, by Morris Goldstein, Donald J. Mathieson, David Folkerts-Landau, Timothy Lane, J. Saúl Lizondo, and Liliana Rojas-Suárez. 1991.

76. China: Economic Reform and Macroeconomic Management, by Mario Blejer, David Burton, Steven Dunaway, and Gyorgy Szapary. 1991.

75. German Unification: Economic Issues, edited by Leslie Lipschitz and Donogh McDonald. 1990.

74. The Impact of the European Community's Internal Market on the EFTA, by Richard K. Abrams, Peter K. Cornelius, Per L. Hedfors, and Gunnar Tersman. 1990.

73. The European Monetary System: Developments and Perspectives, by Horst Ungerer, Jouko J. Hauvonen, Augusto Lopez-Claros, and Thomas Mayer. 1990.

72. The Czech and Slovak Federal Republic: An Economy in Transition, by Jim Prust and an IMF Staff Team. 1990.

Note: For information on the title and availability of Occasional Papers not listed, please consult the IMF *Publications Catalog* or contact IMF Publication Services.